First Sunday: Reflections on Ministry Experiences in the Black Church

Published by Thomas W. Spann in the United States of America.

ISBN 13: 978-1-7352522-2-3
ISBN 10: 1-7352522-2-0

Cover and Interior Design: Brandi K. Etheredge
Copy Editor: Yvette R. Blair-Lavallais

FIRST SUNDAY

Reflections on Ministry Experiences in the Black Church

THOMAS W. SPANN

Dedicated to

Reverend J. H. Neely

Reverend Joseph S. Cooper

TABLE OF CONTENTS

PREFACE

This book has been in the making for over ten years. I have taught sections of it in the course, *Ministry in the Black Church*, which at the time was a foundational course in African American Church Studies at Perkins School of Theology, Southern Methodist University, in Dallas, Texas. The section on the Lord's Supper has given me pause for many years. I have not found any scholarly reflections on it. As I talked about it in one of my Internship seminars, one student stated that I should write on it. And so, I have. I offer Chapter Two as an invitation for further dialogue on this still-practiced ritual in some Black Baptist churches.

I begin the book with Pine Bluff Baptist Church in Karnack, Texas as the window through which I am looking, not only at particular practices and expressions in this church, but in the Black Church in general. Pine Bluff has a special place in my heart since it is the church where I was baptized and acknowledged my call to ministry over fifty years ago. What is said here about Pine Bluff could be said about neighboring rural churches in Karnack or Leigh, Texas, but I use Pine Bluff because of my personal relationship with it and because it has had such a powerful influence in shaping my ministry.

The second chapter focuses on a particular practice that I witnessed each First Sunday at Pine Bluff Baptist Church. It seemed so much a part of the ritual that it has gone practically unnoticed. As I began to think about how Rev. Neely, Rev. Cooper, and the deacons administered the Lord's Supper, I sensed that there was more to it than met the eye. I formed some questions for my own research on this practice. The basic questions were: What is the social origin of this practice? How did the early practitioners understand the theological significance of lifting the

Communion covering like a curtain and holding it up during the entire distribution of the elements? I contacted several pastors, professors, funeral home directors, morticians, and elderly church members, for their assessments of this practice. I concluded that since there were no substantial explanations to my questions, I decided to come up with several hypotheses and use them as the basis of my research and reflections.

Chapter three is an inside look at some of the practices and expressions that can be found in many Black churches. Here I draw on my observations and experiences at a number of churches where I have been a member and a pastoral leader. My interpretation of these practices and expressions are subjective. Many other perspectives or interpretations are possible. I have not attempted to address, by any means, an exhaustive coverage of Black Church cultural expressions and observances. I trust that the ones that I have presented will give the reader a basic understanding of ministry features in Black churches.

The cover photo deserves a comment. I grew up with the impression that this particular scene was never to be photographed. Of course, today there are video recordings of church services that include this scene. Since I never possessed a copy of this scene in my personal collection, I approached a friend and fellow church member, Mr. Wallace Faggett, about taking a picture of it. He stated that he had seen it at New Friendship Missionary Baptist Church in Dallas. I verbally contracted with him to take a picture of it. Later I spoke with the pastor, Rev. Johnny McGee, about getting permission to use it as the cover of the book. He graciously provided me with a letter of consent. Providentially, the photographer is the son of Deacon Edison Faggett who mentored me as I was struggling with my decision to answer God's call to the pulpit ministry at Pine Bluff Baptist Church.

I have included a Study Guide which can be used individually or in small discussion groups. It can be amended by the user in deepening reflections on the significance of many church experiences, practices, and expressions. The user is encouraged to look at her or his church life in light of the guiding questions.

ACKNOWLEDGMENTS

I am thankful for the friendship of Reverend Yvette R. Blair-Lavallais, Senior Pastor of First Christian Methodist Evangelistic Church in Dallas, Texas. She has been a good conversation partner on ministry issues and theological reflection. Many times, when I would spin a story of my life, she would gently encourage me to mark it for the next book.

I am grateful for the support of my St. Luke "Community" United Methodist Church family. Many of them have encouraged me to write. The warm reception that I received from my first book was part of the energy I used to venture into writing this book. I know that I have been blessed by their feedback whenever I have stood before them either as a preacher or a Bible teacher.

I have shared ministry with so many Baptist pastors over the years, and for these experiences I am grateful. I am mindful of some of the practices discussed in this book being carried forth at Mount Sinai Baptist Church in Dallas, Texas, under the leadership of Dr. U.S. Cornelius. I have vivid memories of sharing pulpit ministry with Dr. Cornelius and participating in the leadership of the Communion service with Deacon Paige and Deacon Polk.

I am thankful to all the pastors and lay members who offered me their wisdom about the Lord's Supper. Many of them took the time to send their reflections in writing.

I am thankful for the assistance of Ms. Stephanie Coyle in the Harrison County Clerk's office. When I called the office for help locating some deeds, she quickly responded to my requests.

It goes without saying that I will be forever grateful for the women and men at Pine Bluff Baptist Church who taught, guided, and mentored me along the way. When Pastor Cooper permitted me as a teenager to practice preaching at the end of Sunday School, some core brothers and sisters of the church stayed behind to help me work out my preaching ministry.

I am thankful for the wonderful work done by the copy editor, Yvette R. Blair-Lavallais, and the careful attention to the interior design by Brandi K. Etheredge.

Special thanks to my wife, Cynthia, who read a draft of the book and gave me helpful feedback; and to our two adult children: Monique Redmon and Thomas Spann, Jr. who have always been supportive of their daddy.

EXCERPTS FROM DEEDS

"...Pine Bluff Baptist Church located in Harrison County, Texas ...about seven miles NE from the courthouse in the City of Marshall, Texas, which is known as the 'Sherrod Place,' and being one acre of the Josiah Prewett headright survey in said county, and being the same property described in deed from E. Key to Pine Bluff Baptist Church as the same appears of record in Vol. 77, page 605 of the deed records of Harrison County, Texas.... "(Deed of Records, Vol. 134, page 91, Harrison County, Texas).

❖

"Situated in Harrison County, Texas, and being one acre of the Josiah Prewett survey in Harrison County, Texas, about 7 miles northeast from the court house in the City of Marshall, and being that property described in deed from First National Bank of Marshall, Texas to Pine Bluff Baptist Church dated July 13, 1895 and recorded in Vol.77, page 605 of the deed records of Harrison County, Texas...." (Deed of Records, Vol. 134, page 92, Harrison County, Texas).

❖

"KNOW ALL MEN BY THESE PRESENTS: That I, The First National Bank of Marshall, in the County, of Harrison, and State of Texas, for and in consideration of the sum of One Dollar to me in hand paid, the receipt of which is hereby acknowledged, Have Bargained, Sold, Released, Devised and Conveyed, and by these presents do Bargain—Sell, Release, Devise and Convey unto the Deacons of Pine Bluff Missionary Baptist Church and Society and their successors in office, in trust, however, for the use and benefit of Religious worship, the land and premises described situated, lying and being in the County of Harrison, and State of Texas, about Seven Miles North-East from the Court-House in the City of Marshall in said County, and which is known as the 'Sherrod Place',.... In witness whereof I have set my hand, this 13th, day of July A.D. 1895. First National Bank of Marshall Tex. By E. Key, Prest." (Deed Record 54 Page 172).

Chapter One

PINE BLUFF BAPTIST CHURCH

Background

Pine Bluff Baptist Church is located about seven miles northeast of Marshall on the Stagecoach Road, also called the Pine Bluff Road. It sits down in a flat that once was crowned by towering pines, thus the name Pine Bluff. The Stagecoach Road, along which the church sits, was once the transportation artery between Shreveport, Louisiana and Marshall, Texas. The actual mailing location of the church is Karnack, a small town on Port Caddo Lake.

Many Black churches that were organized after slavery began in brush arbors, a structure built from surrounding tree branches and natural foliage. There are examples of Black churches in the south that were named after surrounding trees such as cedars and oaks; (e.g., Cedar Grove, Live Oak, Oak Grove, Blooming Grove). No surviving records exist to substantiate where the first pioneers of Pine Bluff Baptist Church met. Due to the abundance of pine and sweet gum trees in the area, it is conceivable that Pine Bluff Baptist Church was organized and started in a brush arbor or in an abandoned hay barn owned by an organizing family. Some of the early families in the surrounding area included: the Singletons, the Harrises, the Connors, the Campbells, and the Jacksons.

Pine Bluff Baptist Church was organized in 1869 under the leadership of Reverend George Pritchett and Reverend Sandy Isaacs. Information on Reverend Pritchett could not be found; however, the Federal Census for 1870 approximates Isaacs' birth to be in 1832. Born in Alabama, unable to read or write, he found his way to East Texas, with his wife, Jane. Just four years after the end of slavery in Texas, women and men living in that vicinity answered the call to form themselves into a church. Perhaps somewhat familiar with the doctrines and polity of the White Southern Baptists, the leaders adopted the Baptist principles and form of government. The early pastors of Pine Bluff experienced the pains of enslavement. For example, Reverend William Beckham, born in 1841, became acquainted with both the Free Will Baptists and the Missionary Baptist. His distinction as a leader is that he pastored Pine Bluff for sixteen years. Another pastor, the Reverend J. W. Bailey, was born into the system of slavery near Minden, Louisiana, in 1863. Reverend Bailey published a book entitled "Autobiography of Rev. J. W. Bailey," a copy of which is in the DeGolyer Library at Southern Methodist University in Dallas, Texas.

The early leaders and members of the Pine Bluff Baptist Church were skilled builders, farmers, seamstresses, cooks, and so much more. A later pastor, Reverend William H. Whitten, brought not only experience as a pastor, but he had experience working at a saw mill. As builders and artisans, the early membership dug out a church where they could worship God according to their own liking. The church was built with a basement, a hallway of classrooms and a sanctuary that could seat over two-hundred people. In 1914, Pine Bluff had four-hundred members. The builders of Pine Bluff put their masonry, carpentry, and architectural skills to work just as they had in building the houses, mansions, and churches in and around Marshall. The records of the First United Methodist Church in Marshall indicate that enslaved Africans were involved in its construction.

The genius of Black churches like Pine Bluff in Harrison County, Texas, is that in spite of the fact that Confederates boasted of the county having the largest population of slaves in 1850, Black people came out of the fiery furnace of slavery with a will to organize themselves, to build their own religious institution. Having experienced psychological oppression and physical abuse and limitation of movement, these courageous souls, like the biblical Israelites, had a mind to work and to build a place where they could worship God in spirit and in truth. This was no small undertaking for a people who was told day in and day out that they were chattel, godforsaken, created only to serve the whims and needs of their captors. By the grace of God, they survived not only to tell the story but to institutionalize their convictions about being God's daughters and sons.

It is worth noting that like many formerly enslaved African Americans, the members of Pine Bluff took on the surname of their oppressors, such as Fitzpatrick. In Harrison County the White Fitzpatricks were major owners of enslaved Black flesh. However, instead of naming the church after a White plantation owner, the Blacks along the Stagecoach Road gave their church a name from God's own creation—Pine Bluff. Just as the surrounding pines and other trees were God's handiwork, so were they. Moreover, the early builders and organizers knew that more than trees looked down upon them from a bluff; God, the creator of everything, was watching over them. It is pleasing to imagine that some of these trees made their way into the structure of the church as well as the open slatted pews.

The builders of Pine Bluff built the church on an east-west axis, with the people facing east and the pastor standing in the east to proclaim the Word of God. This orientation was not lost on Masons. Having perhaps a hand in building other churches, the builders of Pine Bluff had an introduction to the significance of east and west in Masonic architecture. East and west both have religious or theological meanings going back to ancient Egypt. In ancient Egyptian religion, east was associated with sunrise, especially with the triumph of the sun-god Ra over the forces of evil in its nightly rotation. In Christian theological imagination, east is associated with the rising sun, resurrection, or new life. West is where the sun sets; it is the entrance into the experience of death. The front cover of many funeral programs indicates the deceased's lifespan by using the images of sunrise (birth) and sunset (death).

As Black churches like Pine Bluff became anchors in the communities where they were planted, people began to identify their residences by using the churches as points of orientation. The moniker of the James Chapel Community had a definite geographical specificity. The James Chapel Community was situated on the old Leigh Road. The Pine Bluff Community indicated houses along the Stagecoach Road as well as those dwellings further back in the woods but close enough to be in walking distance to the church.

Out of necessity churches like St. Paul Baptist Church and Pine Bluff had schools associated with them. In 1874 Pine Bluff organized a Sunday School. It functioned for both religious and public education, teaching children the Bible as well as the well-known three R's—reading, writing, and arithmetic. Children attended school in rural churches in accordance with planting and harvesting seasons. Some of Pine Bluff's early teachers were Professors Cassie (Singleton) Jackson, Mrs. Sarah (Mineweather) Kirks, and Miss Vera Harris. In the 1940s and 50s, Mrs. Lockie Harris, a member of Pine Bluff, had a well-respected, private kindergarten in her home. Education was taken seriously in these church settings. Churches like Pine Bluff that were members of a larger district or state association, e.g., The Texas-Louisiana Baptist Association, reported on the progress of their schools. Attendance records showed that children were called "scholars" instead of students or pupils.

A scholar was a student, not limited to someone who specialized in a narrow field within an academic discipline, or who wrote books. Every person in a Sunday School class or who is enrolled in an educational institution is a scholar. This is an intentional designation that needs to be retrieved. By doing so, we are lifting the expectations of students. Is it possible for us to envision a graduation recognition ceremony in the church or community in which persons are presented as scholars who are going on to make their contribution to society?

An Excursus

Since this study focuses on Pine Bluff Baptist Church in Karnack, Texas, I want to extrapolate three aspects related to the Black Church. My use of the term "Black Church" recognizes that the Black Church is not a monolithic organization. There are many polities, theological beliefs, and worship styles that make up what is called the Black Church. I want, however, briefly to mention the following three aspects related to the historic Black Church: 1) Contributions to the community, 2) Images of the church, and 3) Features of rural churches.

1. Contributions to the Black Community

The contributions of the Black Church are too numerous to provide an exhaustive account. The following is a summary:

- It (the Black Church) reaffirmed on a weekly basis in sermon, song and testimony that Black believers were beloved children of God. Through law and custom African Americans were treated as less than human beings. During slavery, the enslaved were accounted as nothing more than property to be sold and abused and exploited at the will of evil slave holders. We know now that our enslaved ancestors would steal away into the woods and seek solace among each other as they prayed to God to set them free. Deep within they knew that God knew their true names, and in God's presence their dignity and humanity were upheld. The Black preachers assured them that there was a God above who ruled heaven and earth, and the God of Moses had called them daughters and sons of God. Whether in hush harbors (brush arbors), cabins, or, later in organized churches, Black people embraced each other as sisters and brothers with a common sacred parentage.
- It continued to give voice to the deepest aspirations of the people for freedom and justice. The aspirations of Black people in slavery for freedom were expressed in Spirituals. A leading song of freedom was "Go Down, Moses." Even when the Spirituals do not explicitly mention freedom, we know now that certain words were interpreted as carrying deeper meaning. For example, a song about going to Canaan land could be interpreted as life beyond death; however, in the bilingual speech of Africans in slavery it referred to Canada, the land where Black enslaved bodies could be free.

  Alongside the music of the Spirituals were courageous and prophetic voices crying out against the evil system of slavery. These voices included Frederick Douglass, Sojourner Truth, David Walker, Nat Turner, and Gabriel Prosser. After 1865 the aspiration did not cease; the volume may have changed. There was the voice of Bishop Reverdy C. Ransom of the African Methodist Episcopal Church that preached a social gospel and engaged in community activism.

The modern Civil Rights Movement was propelled through the prophetic speeches and sermons of Dr. Martin Luther King, Jr., Rev. Ralph Abernathy, and many others. In theological circles the voice of Dr. James Cone challenged white theology. Pastors like Rev. William Jones, Rev. Dr. Prathia Ann Hall, and Rev. Jeremiah Wright, preached a gospel of freedom and justice that was wholistic, meaning they challenged social inequities but they also challenged the Black Church to get its own house in order, especially on the practice of sexism in the pulpit.

- The Black Church gave people hope in this life while also presenting a grand vision of life in the next world. An overemphasis on heaven led Dr. Benjamin Mays to refer to it as "compensatory religion." Black preachers and choirs did talk and sing a lot about life in the next world, but the church was truly grounded in the daily realities of Black struggle. The struggles and hardships of this life are mentioned in hymns by Thomas Dorsey and Charles Tinsley. Whenever Black people sensed the imbalance in emphasis between heaven and earthly realities, they quoted the line which states: "Some people are so heavenly minded that they are no earthly good." Being heavenly minded is a good outlook but not to the dismissal of seeking to achieve justice on earth.
- The Black Church produced leaders on all fronts who could help aid in the social, economic, political, religious uplift of the people. From the perspective of the Church, there are no self-made leaders. Leaders come out of the communities they serve. The Black Church always had its eyes on potential ministerial candidates, but this did not exclude other vocational callings. Whatever field of endeavor one entered, Black church folks expected the person to work on behalf of the betterment of the community and to exemplify righteous behavior.
- The Black Church provided a space for children and youth to exhibit their gifts and talents. Many noted artists, politicians, and entertainers got their start in the Black Church. A regular feature in Black churches was the participation of children in giving speeches or participating in a dramatic skit during observances like Easter,

Mother's Day, Father's Day, and Christmas. These activities gave many children confidence to stand and deliver in front of an audience.

- The Black Church sponsored schools and colleges for the educational uplift of Black people. Daniel Payne of the African Methodist Episcopal Church (AME) was a guiding force in the establishment of Wilberforce University. Other AME schools include: Allen University in South Carolina, Shorter College in North Little Rock, Arkansas, and Paul Quinn College, established in Waco, Texas but later relocated to Dallas.

  Black Baptists sponsored colleges like Bishop College, founded in Marshall, Texas, in 1881. Bishop College was organized in the basement of the Bethesda Baptist Church. Formerly enslaved persons, with the aid of the community, purchased a 10-acre site of the Holcolmb family, and built a college that was the crown jewel among Black Baptists in Texas.

  The Christian Methodist Episcopal Church sponsored Paine College, Lane College, and Texas College in Tyler.

- The Black Church created mutual aid societies that led to insurance companies and to Black-owned banks. Prior to World War I, Black churches had energized Black people to create and support their own financial institutions. A short list of these banks includes:
  - The Savings Bank of the Grand Fountain United Order of True Reformers
  - The Capital Savings Bank of Washington
  - The Mutual Bank and Trust Company of Chattanooga
  - The Wage Earner's Bank in Savannah, Georgia
  - The Citizens and Southern Bank in Philadelphia
  - The St. Luke Penny Savings Bank, led by Maggie Lena Walker
  - The One-Cent Savings and Trust Company Bank.

  From the heroic work of women and men to help establish economic centers in the Black community, some contemporary African American owned banks have emerged. These banks have included:
  - One United Bank
  - Citizens Trust Bank

- Seaway Bank
- Liberty Bank
- Industrial Bank.

Some churches ventured into the credit union side of finance. Two Black Baptist churches that did this are: Mount Olive in Arlington, Texas, and Good Street Baptist Church in Dallas, Texas.

- The Black Church provided organized opportunities for Black people to convene themselves for religious, political, social, and cultural enhancement.

Pine Bluff Baptist Church in Karnack, Texas, may not boast of being able to check off all the particular contributions listed above. It, however, served, and continues to serve the community. It has been a healing space where people whose lives have been ruptured and displaced by forces beyond their control could come and find healing through the arts of music, prayers, praise, preaching, and shouting.

Pine Bluff, like all historic organized Black churches, gave women and men their dignity back on Sunday when they were greeted by titles and offices, or generally recognized as an elder in the community.

Pine Bluff could not be described as an activist or liberationist church in the sense of being on the front line to wage battles against structural injustices in the school system, financial community, or the political arena. Church members who left town following school to seek employment in other cities or states, or to further their education, took with them the values and spiritual resources of the church. Whatever contributions they have made to the new places where they set down roots, and to their new communities of faith can be traced back to the moral and spirituals teachings of Pine Bluff Church.

2. Images of the Black Church

I want briefly to comment on three images of the Black Church.

- Keeper of African American History

The story of African Americans' achievements and struggles for justice and equality is intricately connected with the church. The church was the hub of community life. Education, community gatherings, economic initiatives, and therapeutic experiences, have their early genesis in the

Black Church. When politicians wanted an audience to present their candidacy, they came to the church. Where there were efforts to raise money for a good cause, the initiators of the cause came to the church for help. Black churches themselves stood as living lessons of creativity, initiative, pride, and resilience. The history of Black America cannot be justly told without referencing the Black Church as the genesis and keeper of that story.

At a local level, not many individual Black churches have dedicated themselves to archiving the stories and records of the church. Few churches have book-length histories from its beginning to the present. Too often important documents, papers, and church programs, bulletins, and obituaries are discarded. It might be better for original copies of church documents to be filed in the office of the church's attorney or another secure depository, so that when a holder of the church minutes or other documents gets out of sorts with the pastor or officers or some other member, the documents are not withheld, or, worse, thrown out in either anger or ignorance. When family members of a deceased church secretary or any holder of church records come across papers related to the business of the church, they should contact the pastor or officers to arrange for the return of the records. The elders who are viewed as seasoned saints of wisdom are not systematically interviewed for their memories and historical memories and artifacts. Many Black churches celebrate their anniversaries with emphasis on raising money and putting on a program, but the written history of the church is confined to one or maybe two pages inside the anniversary booklet. We must become better stewards of our history so that our children and grandchildren may have a light to inspire them.

- An Army or Soldiers

Given the philosophy of non-violence associated with the Civil Rights Movement, the Peace Movement of the 1960's, and the rise in gun violence and homicides, this militaristic image of the church is not as prevalent as it once was. It, nevertheless, is an image in the collection of church portraits.

While the metaphor of army or soldiers may be sidelined because of the suggestion of violence or military force, the reality is that Black

Americans continue daily to engage the forces of systemic racism. The summons to keep up the struggle or to find a good fight and get involved, or, as Congressman John Lewis often said, get in some "good trouble," are versions of being engaged in a battle for our civil and human rights.

Black preachers used Ephesians chapter 6 to call Christians to be properly suited against the enemies of righteousness. Some well-known songs appealed to the image of the church as an army of the Lord. These include: "I Shall Not Be Moved," "I Am on the Battlefield," and "We Are Soldiers."

• A Spiritual Home/Family

This is a bedrock metaphor for the church. Through Christ's sacrifice and our common heritage of struggle, Black Christians saw each other as sisters and brothers. The invitation following the sermon always included membership in the family of God. Many church visitors seek a place where they can feel at home, where there is genuine love and health in the community.

A spiritual home or church family is a place where joys and struggles and hardships of life are shared and borne together. Members support one another in their walk with Christ as well as in their personal lives. A family is a place of love, where members are encouraged to do and be their best, where wise guidance and instructions are given. Membership in the family of God crowns each human life with sacred dignity and worth. No one is marginalized or treated as second-class. A church family is a community where the truth is spoken in love.

Like any family unit, there are secrets in churches that can disable growth and truthfulness. Secrets lead to lying, cover-ups, and triangulation. Moreover, church family secrets can become generational, thus continuing a legacy of not dealing honestly with issues that compromise inter-personal relationships. At the core of many nagging church conflicts are secrets that have not been dealt with.

Of the images presented, Pine Bluff Baptist Church may be described as being 1) a spiritual home/family and 2) a hospital for the sick. Throughout the week, members cared for each other; they prayed together; they encouraged one another, especially the school children. When there was domestic difficulty in a family, church members, some who may have been related to either the husband or the wife, would intervene, as appropriate. They offered counsel and sometimes stiff words of correction to an offending party. In the rhythm of church and community life, children were protected; the elders were respected; the sick were cared for, often at home; the dying were surrounded with the songs and prayers of spiritual sisters and brothers.

3. Features of Rural Church Life

• Traditionally, rural life moved at a slower pace than in bustling towns and cities.

The rhythm of life was set to the planting and harvesting seasons, the opening and closing of the school year, and the movement through the church's own calendar year. The rural church calendar included observances such as: Church Anniversary, Pastor's Anniversary, Choir Anniversary, Black History Month, and Annual Revival.

In rural churches time was not so much governed by the clock on the wall but by worship leaders' internal clock which determined when it was time to start a worship service. The depth of the people's experiences with the Spirit taught them not to put too much confidence in the clock. Worship began when the people's spirits were ready to enter into the joys of the Lord. As was often the case, worship lasted for two or three hours; the preacher was encouraged to take his time in breaking the bread of life. After the benediction there was no rush to leave. Fellowshipping with one another was an extension of worship.

• Rural churches were not so large that people did not know each other.

Many of these communities of faith were largely made up of core families. They knew each other in family gatherings, school, work, and living in the same vicinity.

When a parent needed to borrow an item from a neighbor, a child might be sent to ask for the requested item in the name of the parent. Sharing what each one had was central to community life. It might be the case that one day the person who is giving might be in need of a favor tomorrow.

Rural life meant a dependence on family and friends. An example is the collective work during hog killing season. When it was cold enough to butcher hogs, the men came together to help a neighbor with the entire process, while the women prepared the wash pot for boiling, and later, cooking. At the end of the process, meat was stored in a smokehouse. Meat was also shared with other families in the neighborhood. During the upcoming weeks, cooks made hog-head cheese, crackling bread, and cleaned and cooked chitterlings.

Another example of community assistance in a time of need is when a family's well would go dry. Friends would come and help dig until a new source of water was found. This was done by tying a rope around a man who went down into the well with a small shovel, pick, and bucket. When the bucket was filled with mud, other men at the mouth of the well would draw the bucket up, empty it, and send it back down. The spirit of cooperation was guided by neighborly love but also by the reality that it might be someone else's dry well tomorrow.

- In rural Black communities, family was not limited to biological or blood line.

Sociologists refer to this extended family dynamic as "fictive kin." Beyond a child's actual aunts and uncles or siblings, there may be several other people in the family called by special family titles.

In this regard, children belonged to the whole community. There were other mothers and fathers who watched, taught, and disciplined children. When a child was granted permission to go and play with a neighboring child, it was understood in the community that the mother or father of the child being visited had a responsibility equal to that of any loving, caring, parent. It was often the case in rural Black communities for a child who got in trouble to be disciplined at a friend's home and at one's own home, because the mothers communicated with each other about the child's behavior.

- Rural life meant that people had to be creative or inventive. There was not always the money to go into town to buy what was desired. Out of necessity came the tools, toys, or clothing that was needed or desired. Creativity and inventiveness led to beautiful quilts being made. Some parents made dresses for their daughters. Children would make toys like dolls, kites, bow and arrows, and games, to occupy their time.

- A basic feature of rural church life was storytelling. Of course, today children and youth have access to various forms of social media and personal cell phones. The dynamic of family life today is centered around technology and television. In an earlier period in rural community life, children grew up listening to stories—family history, personal experiences of the parent/storyteller, and imaginative tales.

The emphasis on storytelling was key to the calling of a pastor. A key question that the community raised was, "Can he tell the story?" Telling the gospel story meant the oral ability to connect the gospel with the people's lives in the classic tradition of high emotional excitement and vocal creativity.

Pine Bluff Baptist Church experienced many of these features, and many others. Because the church was, for many years, a first and third Sunday church, the pastor had another church. This meant that the pastor was not readily accessible, except for a funeral or a church business meeting. One of Pine Bluff's pastors lived in the city of Marshall while also leading a church in Vivian, Louisiana. In the absence of the pastor, the church was run by the chairman of the deacon board.

In its early years, Pine Bluff Baptist Church, like many rural churches, did not provide a pension plan or standard allowances for the pastor. This meant that ministers worked beyond the expected retirement years. The annual Pastor's Anniversary not only celebrates the work of the minister for the year, but it was also a means of supplementing the salary of the pastor. Many rural pastors became evangelists out of financial need as well as to share the gospel in other settings.

Like many rural churches, Pine Bluff had a standing Building Fund. The church did not have a standard college scholarship fund, but it was sure to have a building fund. This account was used to pay for repairs to the church or add on to the existing building. Except for installing indoor restrooms and adding a small foyer with an awning, to my knowledge, the physical structure of the church has remained the same before and after it was bricked.

Missionary, Institutional, and Masonic

Pine Bluff Baptist Church was organized prior to the Missionary Baptist movement among freed African Americans. The three impactful Black Baptist Conventions formed between 1880 and 1893 were: the Foreign Mission Baptist Convention of the United States, the American National Baptist Convention, and the Baptist National Educational Convention. In the original deed of the church (1895), Pine Bluff is listed as Pine Bluff Missionary Baptist Church and Society. The reference to Society possibly meant the Missionary Society led by the women of the church. Moreover, this preferably was a reference to the Mutual Aid Society, a feature of many Black churches. Through this Society the sick were helped; families were given assistance in burying the dead; money was lent in times of need; and the elderly were given medical care and support.

Another movement that was embraced by some Black Baptist churches at the turn of the Twentieth Century was the Social Gospel Movement. Convinced that being involved in the wholistic uplift of Black people is the church's ministry, many Black churches embraced a more inclusive gospel. Churches that engaged in social service or welfare ministries were called Institutional churches. Churches carrying this label emphasized Sunday Schools, built recreational spaces, sponsored literacy groups and libraries, offered food and shelter, vocational classes, music, the arts and clubs for girls and boys.

Baptist churches that kept the word "Institutional" after the waning of the social gospel movement are continuing a legacy of social justice ministry. Two examples of contemporary churches that bear this name include: Olivet Institutional Baptist Church in Cleveland, Ohio, and First Institutional Baptist Church in Phoenix, Arizona.

Whether a Baptist church was Missionary or Institutional, an organization that stood alongside the church was the Masonic Lodge. In 1957 Pine Bluff sold a half-acre of land to Campbell Masonic Lodge #548. A lodge hall was built just to the south of the church. Most of the Lodge members were Pine Bluff members. Lodge members included: Edward Blackmon, Ennis Powell, William Jones, Estra Key, Obie Tippens, Doris Johnson, and Anderson Sheppard. Campbell Masonic Lodge was part of a long tradition in Black Masonry, going back to its founder, Prince Hall.

Black Masons created for themselves a sense of pride, accomplishments, and cadre of leaders that could only be equaled in the Black Church. In this regard, Prince Hall Masons and the Church, though different in aims, functioned to provide social services and financial assistance to members. Lodge members were encouraged to keep up their dues, because the resources of the Lodge went to assist family members in burying the dead, helping members in need, and supporting college students. Many Black churches called on a Masonic Lodge to lead in the observance of the laying of a cornerstone. Many older Black churches will have the name of the particular lodge that assisted in laying the cornerstone.

While Prince Hall Lodges were made up of men, the group for women was called Order of the Eastern Star. Like the Masons, Eastern Star members had their secret symbols, initiation rites and codes, but their community outreach was similar to the Masons. A core principle of both Masons and Eastern Star members was mutual assistance in a time of need. It was a popular belief that Masons, when stranded on the highway or in need, could give a special sign to indicate their fraternal status, and receive help from a mutual member.

Preparations for First Sunday

In the rural community in which I grew up, the importance of Sunday was reflected in activities the day before. Sunday was the Lord's Day, and washing laundry, ironing clothes, mowing yards, getting one's hair done, and, to some degree, cooking, were done on Saturday. Saturday's activities were done with an eye on keeping Sunday holy. Generally, most Black people in the community waited until Saturday to go into town to shop, browse, take a breather, or visit with friends and neighbors on the courthouse square.

As indicated, clothes were washed or ironed and laid out on Saturday in preparation for Sunday. We had school clothes, play clothes, and work clothes, but we also had church clothes and church shoes. We signified the importance of Sunday by not wearing church clothes and shoes on other days unless there was a very special occasion.

In our home we did not watch cartoon television shows on Sunday morning. If there was any music to be played, it had to be church music, and when the television was turned on, it was turned to a church program.

My father would take me with him some Saturdays as he visited neighbors. I observed that while they talked generally about their lives, politics, and family, they would also discuss a Bible lesson. Before parting, I noticed that they begged one another's pardon. This last act caught my attention because it was connected with getting ready to eat the bread of the Lord and to drink from the common cup. Doubtless, my father and his friends took seriously Paul's admonition to examine themselves so as not to eat and drink unworthily (I Corinthians 11:28-29). In the act of pardoning one another, my father and his friends were making sure that they did not come to the Lord's Table out of fellowship with one another.

First Sunday had a special attraction because it was the day when the members showed their love for God and one another by drinking from the common cup and eating the holy bread, symbols of Christ's body. In many rural households with a well, a pail of water was kept in the kitchen. In the pail was a tin dipper from which anyone could drink. Drinking together from the common cup acknowledged the oneness of the family of God which was made possible by Christ's gracious sacrifice.

First Sunday drew members far and wide who may not have attended worship on previous Sundays. At the Lord's Table was a visible and vivid reminder that God did for us in Christ what we could not do for ourselves. No matter how smart or strong we might think we are, there is nothing in us that could have equaled the sin-defeating act of God's love on the cross.

Women and men who could barely read knew the story surrounding the Lord's Supper. That story appealed to their desire to be people who lived pleasing lives in God's sight. Whatever disagreements or unhealthy relational tensions there were between members could be reconciled at the Lord's Table. Christ's invitation was to come and be made whole. God's love drew church members to the Lord's Table as nothing else could. I have known church members who were alcoholics during the week but would sober up and dress up to come to the church to partake of the Lord's Supper.

First Sunday drew people because at the Lord's Table was the intersection of the present life and a future hope. The worst sinner in the church did not want to die having missed the Lord's Supper. The bread and cup reflected salvation both in the present age and in the future. The ethical implication for present living was to be in a right relationship with one's neighbor. The same ethic of justice had implications for eternal life.

Why does First Sunday hold such an attraction?

First Sunday is significant because it is the time when the community gathers to renew their participation in Christ's redeeming power.

First Sunday is significant because the community shares in the redemptive story of Christ's great act of love. The story is not only in the Bible; it is not only recited by the preacher. The people get to live into the story at the table of the Lord.

First Sunday is a day in which the community affirms that the ground is level at the cross. As the elders at Pine Bluff would say, "There's no big I and little you." We are all precious in God's sight. Titles, degrees, and pretension to self-importance are done away with at the Lord's Table. All who partake come as sinners in need of God's grace.

Personal Memories

Revivals/Baptisms

Revival meetings are not unlike the old southern campground meetings in which there was powerful preaching, great singing, and intense emotional responses. A revival had as its intended purpose to renew the church's faith and commitment to Christ. Emphasis, however, was on inviting persons to accept Christ as their Savior. To revive is to make alive again. Revival meetings assumed that a church can lose some of its energy for doing God's will. The people and the preacher can sometimes grow weary in carrying on the work of God. The revival meeting was looked to as a source of inspiration, almost at midpoint in the calendar year. While each Sunday's worship experience had the same purpose, the spirit of the revival anticipated a wider swath of invitations and responses. In the church's regular Sunday morning worship, the same people, for the most part, attended and participated. However, the spirit of revival appealed to both the saved and the unsaved: to the saved for further growth in faith; to the unsaved to turn one's life over to God.

Perhaps a good analogy for a revival is the renewal of marriage vows. A good marriage could continue without the ceremony of renewal, but the act of renewal itself adds something new to the marriage. Revival is like renewing the vows believers made when they were brought into the family of God. The vows don't change but people do. So, it is important to establish a sacred beachhead where, as in marriage, the church can enter anew into the covenant with each other and Christ and look forward together to God's brand new future.

In addition to seeking converts for Christ, the revival meeting overall is an opportunity for relationships between church members to improve or grow. A never-failing appeal in many churches is for unity or oneness in mind and purpose. A willingness to overcome internal discord and personal conflicts make revivals meaningful all the more. Being out of fellowship with a fellow believer is to be out of fellowship with Christ. The hope of revival is that the Spirit of the Living God will move persons to seek forgiveness, healing, and restoration, with each other and God.

Given the fact that there were so many churches holding revivals, they were often held the same week. In some cases, when one revival ended, another one was being held the following week somewhere in the community. The seasonal window of opportunity was fairly narrow, thus leading to concurrent and back-to-back revivals. Pine Bluff Baptist Church held its annual revival the week leading up to the third Sunday in August. In its early history this was due to the planting and harvesting season, but it also took in consideration the opening of school in September.

The harvesting season is important to mention here because, while the guest evangelist was given an honorarium, the people, on the last night, would often give the evangelist fruits and vegetables as expressions of their appreciation. Church members who did not have a lot of money to give, gave out of their gardens and fields what would be the equivalent of monetary donations.

The timing of Pine Bluff's revival in August placed it as the concluding highlight of summer activities. At the end of the school year in May, we looked forward to summer fun, especially church-wide celebration of freedom from slavery in Texas on June 19th, also known as Juneteenth. For several years, the church met on Juneteenth on Calvin Jackson's property, about a mile further down the Pine Bluff Road (Stagecoach Road). The children played baseball in the field, ate watermelons, drank red soda water, and there was plenty of fried chicken, vegetables, and cakes. Being in a truly rural environment, the Jacksons lived with no electricity or running water or motorized transportation. Mr. Jackson grew crops in the field, raised animals and chickens, and picked berries and wild grapes. Sometimes community neighbors who could not get to the store in town would go to the Jacksons to get fresh vegetables.

Following Juneteenth, individual families celebrated the Fourth of July in their homes or with neighbors; sometimes there was an organized gathering at a local park. July Fourth, like Juneteenth, was marked with fun, food, family, and fellowship. A staple for this celebration was homemade ice cream.

So, the summer schedule, in addition to whatever trips or vacations families may take, consisted of Juneteenth and Fourth of July celebrations, capped off, so to speak, with a week-long revival in August.

Informal assessments of revivals had to do with the quality of the preaching and the number of candidates for baptism. It was a fairly standard expectation that when children reached the age of twelve or not much later than thirteen, they were to be candidates for baptism. Based on the Sunday School roster, it was common knowledge who potential candidates were. There were, however, youths who did not attend Sunday School but whose status was known by church members. It was the duty of parents or guardians to encourage potential candidates to attend the revival meeting. When this parental duty was treated lightly, deacons and missionary sisters approached parents and children about the urgency of this spiritual decision.

In preparation for the revival, Pine Bluff had a tradition of conducting a week-long prayer meeting. The seriousness of the revival was undergirded by the seriousness of prayer. Prayers were for the efficacy of the preaching as well as for the receptivity of the invitation to give one's heart to God and to continue to grow in love and fellowship with one another and

God. Those who gathered for the week of prayer did so expecting the power of God to be manifested in all the acts of praise. The hope was that no one left the revival the same way they came. It was one thing to have a good time in the Lord and another for hearts to be changed.

In truth, the weekly Wednesday night prayer meeting would have been sufficient, but the saints knew that there had to be a night of prayer for every night of the revival. In the language of the church, "The devil is busy," therefore, it takes persistence and power to remove every obstacle to the blessings that God has for individuals and for the church.

The revivalist or evangelist was selected by the pastor. This person was selected by the pastor for his reputation as a powerful preacher. A revivalist with an awesome preaching reputation would sometimes be introduced with a nickname, such as, a preaching machine, God's special thunderbolt, fireball of a preacher, or gospel giant.

Most of the revivalists were also active pastors. The revivalist's own church considered it a part of their mission to extend the gospel by giving the pastor the time to spread the gospel. If the revivalist was someone from out-of-town, there might be an occasion when he needed to return to his home base during the day, if possible, to conduct a funeral, or attend a pressing engagement that would allow him time to get back for the revival.

A tradition at Pine Bluff was for potential candidates for baptism to sit on the front pew, known as the mourner's bench. Behind the mourner's bench sat the saints of the church, mostly women, who prayed and sang, with the sincere hope that the Spirit would move each child or youth to respond to the evangelist's invitation to accept Christ as their personal Lord and Savior. Each potential candidate was guided to kneel at the bench and give prayerful consideration to hearing God's voice of invitation to turn their life over to God. The gathered community had an expectation for the potential candidate, but the decision had to be a personal one; no one could make this crucial, life-changing decision for the child. A child or youth left on the mourner's bench this year would return next year with the hope of making that personal decision. When a personal decision was made to give one's hand to the preacher and heart to God, there was great rejoicing.

The revival ended on Friday night with the whole church looking forward to the coming Sunday. Sunday was both the time for baptisms and celebrating Big Day or homecoming. Big Day was special because former members and visiting churches came to celebrate in an afternoon service. Farmers with horse-drawn wagons parked on the side of the road to sell food. Cars crowded both the church lot and along the road in both directions. There was plenty of food as people gathered to eat and fellowship between the baptism service and the three o'clock afternoon service.

At the conclusion of the morning service, candidates for baptism changed into appropriate clothing and were wrapped in a white sheet. The pastor and the deacons led the procession from the church to the baptismal site across the road and into the woods. Songs like "Take Me to the Water" and "Wade in the Water," were lyrical escorts to the pool. The wooded baptism site had been dug many years ago and was boarded to hold water that ran down from a natural outlet under a rock. This natural spout was often used by neighbors when water wells ran dry.

Upon arrival to the site, one of the deacons would wade into the pool with a long stick to measure the depth. The pastor on one side and the deacon on the other would baptize each candidate using the classic Trinitarian formula: In the name of God the Father, Christ the Son, and the Holy Spirit.

Following the baptism ceremony, the candidates and witnesses returned to the church for a festive meal. This was followed by the afternoon service in which the baptism candidates sat on the front row as members of Christ's holy church.

Church Covenant

In the afternoon following baptism, the pastor called the baptized persons' attention to the Church Covenant. This was an oversized document on the wall in the choir stand at Pine Bluff. Baptized candidates were not required to memorize it. The Covenant has been posted in the same location at the church for over fifty years. The Church Covenant, second only to the Bible, stands over the congregation as a moral guide and spiritual reminder of the commitments that were made upon being received into the fellowship of the church. Even when the pulpit Bible was closed, the Church Covenant remained an uncovered or unclosed witness to the highs and lows of the church's life.

The Covenant was often appealed to when there were disagreements or the appearance of differences that could not be reconciled between members or between the pastor and church leaders. The appeal did not always bring about the desired outcome; it, nevertheless, acted as judge of church behavior.

The text of the Church Covenant

Having been led, as we believe by the Spirit of God, to receive the Lord Jesus Christ as our Savior and, on profession of our faith, having been baptized in the name of the Father, and of the Son and of the Holy Spirit, we do now, in the presence of God and this assembly, most solemnly and joyfully enter into covenant with one another as one body in Christ.

We engage, therefore, by the aid of the Holy Spirit, to walk together in Christian love; to strive for the advancement of this church, in knowledge, holiness and comfort; to promote its prosperity and spirituality; to sustain its worship, ordinances, discipline, and doctrines; to contribute cheerfully and regularly to the support of the ministry, the expenses of the church, the relief of the poor, and the spread of the Gospel through all nations.

We also engage to maintain family and secret devotions; to religiously educate our children; to seek the salvation of our kindred and acquaintances; to walk circumspectly in the world; to be just in our dealings, faithful in our engagements, and exemplary in our deportment; to avoid all tattling, backbiting and excessive anger; to abstain from the sale of, and use of intoxicating drinks as a beverage; and to be zealous in our efforts to advance the kingdom of our Savior.

We further engage to watch over one another in brotherly love; to remember one another in prayer; to aid one another in sickness and distress, to cultivate Christian sympathy in feeling and Christian courtesy in speech; to be slow to take offense, but always ready for reconciliation and mindful of the rules of our Savior, to secure it without delay.

We moreover engage that when we remove from this place, we will, as soon as possible, unite with some other church where we can carry out the spirit of this covenant and the principles of God's word.

When John Newton Brown composed this statement in the 1850s, African Americans in the south were still in the bonds of chattel slavery. There is no indication in this document that the broader context of Baptist behavior was institutionalized slavery. Many Baptists were slaveholders and did not see the incongruence between faith in Christ and the degrading practice of human bondage. Moreover, at the time of the composition of this document, Blacks were not equal members of the Southern Baptist churches. From the perspective of enslaved persons, how could one "walk circumspectly in the world" while denying that all persons, inclusive of Africans, were equally created by God and were recipients of "inalienable rights?" What did it mean to enslaved Africans for slaveholders "to be just in our dealings, faithful in our engagements, and exemplary in our deportment"? In a socially constructed system of white superiority and Black inferiority, what did it mean "to aid one another in sickness and distress, to cultivate Christian sympathy in feeling and Christian courtesy in speech"? White Baptists who entered into this covenant did so with the clear understanding that this agreement was solely among themselves. Social custom and law forbade even Christians from treating Black people as if they had rights equal to that of everyone in the church or nation.

When Black Baptists organized themselves into conventions in the late nineteenth century, they adopted this Church Covenant in its entirety. No attempt was made to amend or modify the document so as to accord with their struggles for equality and justice. It would have been appropriate for Black Baptists to take a more progressive stand against racism while advocating ethical interpersonal relations.

The Classic Deacon's Prayer

Whenever Deacon Edward Blackmon or Deacon Wright prayed as a part of opening devotion at Pine Bluff Baptist Church, each of them, and many other deacons and laypersons, offered the same prayer, almost verbatim. It was so impressive in its images and repetition, that I, along with many other children, memorized it. We knew which petition or phrase was coming next. The prayer as I remembered it is as follows:

> *Almighty and all-wise God our heavenly Father, 'tis once more and again that a few of your humble children come knee-bent and body-bowed around your throne of grace to call upon your holy name. We come as empty pitchers before a full fountain, ready to be filled. We don't come before you for any outside show, form, or fashion, as in this unfriendly world. We come to worship you in spirit and in truth, and to turn unto you some true and humble thanks.*
>
> *We thank you that you watched over us all night while we slumbered and slept. We thank you that the bed we slept on was not our cooling board. We thank you that the sheet we slept on was not our winding sheet. Early this morning, while we slept in the very image of death, you touched us with the finger of love and our eyes flew open to behold a day that we have never seen before and that we will never see again. We thank you that the blood was still running warm in our veins and that we had a reasonable portion of health and strength. We were able to get up this morning clothed in our right mind. We thank you for our spared lives, for, Master, since last we met, many have been snatched from the land of the living and gone to try a world unknown. But through your goodness and mercy, you have seen fit to leave us here where we can pick and choose our own praying ground. We thank you that you have allowed our golden moments to roll on just a little while longer. O Lord, continue to have mercy, for mercy suits our case. We thank you for protecting us from dangers seen and unseen.*
>
> *O Lord, continue to throw around us your strong arms of protection. Bind us together in one band of Christian love. Help us to feel one another's love—the kind of love that runs from heart*

to heart and from breast to breast. Strengthen us where we are weak; build us up where we are torn down; and prop us up on every leaning side.

O Lord, take the reins of our minds, place them on heaven and heavenly divine things. Search our hearts and if you find anything contrary to your divine will, just move it from us, as far as the east is from the west. O cast it into the sea of forgetfulness where it will never rise against us at the judgment bar.

Now, Lord, you know our hearts; you know our heart's desire. You know all about us because you made us.

Now, Lord, one more kind favor I ask: remember the one who is to stand in John's shoes to declare your word between the living and the dead. Your word is sharper than any two-edged sword. It goes down between the marrow and the bone. O stand by him, Lord. Strengthen him where he is weak and build him up where he is torn down. O let him down into the deep treasures of your word so that he might proclaim a true and mighty word.

And now, Lord, when this your humble servant is through praying down here, when I have to stack hymn books and Bibles and stick my sword in the sand of time to study war no more; O I pray, Lord, that you would meet me in my dying hour. Meet me at the river and cross me over in a calm time into that land where the wicked shall cease from troubling and the weary shall be at rest, where everyday will be Sunday and Sabbath will have no end. This is your servant's prayer in the name of Jesus, Amen, and thank God.

This prayer has been in the worship vocabulary of the Black Church for well over a century, and is still alive today. From south to north, from coast to coast, this prayer is as familiar in Baptist circles as is the Lord's Prayer. This spiritual offering came into existence through communal working and re-working of the images, as formerly enslaved Africans built their own prayer tradition. A careful reading of it leads to the conclusion that this is a communal endeavor, crafted by gifted orators. Perhaps as one person was praying, the congregation would add words or phrases that merged into the body of the prayer. In truth, this is the people's prayer.

It is characterized by vivid images and metaphors that bear witness to the users' knowledge of the Bible. Some of the images come out of their life experiences, such as cooling board and winding sheet. Grounded in communal gratitude for life, this prayer moves toward life with God in the hereafter. The inevitability of death and gratitude to God for life are motivators of the request for God to forgive their sins and help them to stand up straight.

It has to be acknowledged that this prayer has brought us a mighty long way. A question that has to be asked is: Is this prayer relevant today? Something has to be said for the fact that it is still being used in some traditional Black Baptist worship experiences. Use does not necessarily equate to relevance. Perhaps the question of relevance invites a history lesson with young people on the ways and means that our foreparents used spirituality to survive the harshness of their lives. It is understandable if modern worshipers have a sense of embarrassment by hearing a prayer that comes out of our ancestors' struggle; nevertheless, we have a responsibility to remember our spiritual genius, and pass it on to the next generation. It will be up to them to decide how to respond to this treasured cultural heirloom.

Images of Jesus in the Church

In the King James Version of the Bible that was used by Pine Bluff Church members were paintings of Moses, Jesus, and angels, who were the color of the artist who painted them. At Pine Bluff, white images of Jesus were in front of the pulpit in an enclosed glass frame, on hand fans, and on classroom walls. These images in Black churches were signs of the depth of theological miseducation and social appropriation of White racism. Black people did not, en masse, challenge segregation or racist laws in the south until the confrontation in Montgomery in 1955, when Rosa Parks was arrested for refusing to give up her bus seat to a White man. That incident sparked the Civil Rights Movement of the 1950s and 60s. Segregation laws and perceived superiority of White people were given theological and political support in the dominant paintings of Jesus and other biblical characters. In other words, white supremacy wrapped itself in sacred garb by assigning whiteness to God, Jesus, and the angels. This false theology created psychological distortions for Blacks and whites for centuries. To attend a Black church and perceive God and angels as white was the height of spiritual aberration. Black Christians digested these images as a part of religious education and did not question the racism behind white images of Jesus. Consequently, the spiritual damage led to the passivity which did not threaten the unjust structures of society. To do so was perceived as challenging the Divine.

For Blacks to perceive of Jesus as Black was initially both a spiritually herculean task and a soul-disturbing experience. The spiritual torture must have been tremendous when Black artists began to break the hold of white supremacy by painting Jesus as Black. This was not an easy change for many Black churches to accept. Centuries of psychological distortions backed up by preachers and theologians did not crumble over night. There was resistance in some Black churches to images of Jesus as Black as there was in White seminaries to a Black theology. Even when there was gradual acceptance that Blacks had as much freedom to see Jesus and God through their own cultural eyes, there was still the matter of racist paintings built into stain-glassed windows and other spaces in churches. Moreover, when Black artists drew images of Jesus, Jesus still had, in many portraits, long flowing curly hair, and brown-skinned angels sprouted white wings. The residue of racism is hard to overcome in architecture and in art.

While color portraits of divine images carry psychological impact, another issue is that of seeing God in living Black or brown skin persons. African Americans read in the Bible that God made humanity in God's image. They read in the gospels that Jesus said, "The kingdom of God is within you." The spiritual question is: Can we see, embrace, and love the God who is in us? God cannot be present in all flesh until God is accepted and seen in Black women and men.

Theological systems that supported the enslavement of Africans were created by White men who saw themselves as chosen by God to dominate the world. These are systems that must be challenged. To question theological systems built on White racism is not to question or challenge God; to question them is the highest expression of faith. Black faith accepts the biblical insight that "out of one blood God created all nations to dwell on the face of the earth" (Acts 17:26). Ultimately, a mature Black faith says, in the words of Jesus, "God is Spirit, and to worship God is worship in spirit and in truth" (John 4:24). From this theological wisdom, White people are not divinely ordained to be superior; Black people are not divinely ordained to be inferior, and God cannot be captured or controlled by any human system that makes oppression and systemic injustice synonymous with God's will for human life.

A major attempt to address the prevailing notion that major biblical figures were all Europeans was the release of *The Original African Heritage Study Bible*, edited by Dr. Cain Hope Felder. Prior to Felder's Bible, as I have indicated, the major Bible publishers, especially of the King James Version, had illustrations or paintings of biblical characters who were Europeans. In addition to insightful commentaries, this Bible includes photographs of Black people. By identifying biblical characters with African peoples, Felder broke a major link in the web of internalized oppression.

Consistent with Dr. Felder's work there grew a body of literature that appropriated the hermeneutic of Africentrism in biblical exegesis. Some of these important works are listed below.

- *Troubling Biblical Waters* by Cain Hope Felder
- *Those Preachin' Women*, edited by Ella Mitchell
- *The Black Presence in the Bible* by Walter McCray
- *Black Characters and References of the Holy Bible* by F. S. Rhodes
- *Black Biblical Studies: An Anthology of Charles B. Copher*
- *Afrocentric Sermons* by Kenneth Waters
- *The Recovery of Black Presence* by Randall Bailey and Jacqueline Grant, editors
- *Africa and the Africans in the Old Testament* by David Tuesday Adamo
- *The Africana Bible: Reading Israel's Scriptures From Africa and The African Diaspora*, Hugh R. Page, Jr., General Editor
- *True to Our Native Land: An African American New Testament Commentary*, Brian Blount, General Editor.

There is a collection of paintings in which the Mafa people in northern Cameroon are acting out various scenes of the gospel. This collection of pictures is titled: Life of Jesus Mafa: Scenes of the Gospel Dramatized by the Mafa People in Northern Cameroun.

Protocols

Protocols are expectations that govern an organization. Protocols may be written or oral. Protocol in some churches is learned by observation and participation rather than by verbal instruction.

The protocols stated below represent a collection of expectations I learned at Pine Bluff and other churches where I have participated.

- Never enter a pulpit without being invited by the pastor. If you are visiting, go to the church office and make your presence known.
- If you are seated in the pulpit, stand when a guest pastor or the pastor enters the pulpit after service has begun.
- Never address the pastor by first name in public.
- Don't speak disparagingly about another pastor or church in front of lay members.
- When giving a gift to a married pastor, give something of equal value or acknowledgment to the spouse.
- Children are not allowed to run or play in the pulpit.
- Wait for the pastor to enter before starting a service or get permission to begin without the pastor present.
- In listing or calling the names of ministers, including assistant or associate ministers in a church, the pastor's name is listed or called first.
- Following the sermon and other post-sermon activities, it is expected that the last word is from the pastor. It is highly unusual for someone to get up after the pastor has given closing remarks.
- After the sermon has been delivered by the pastor or a guest minister, do not get up and try to re-teach or re-preach the sermon.
- Smoking in the church building and on the grounds is prohibited.
- The Communion table is holy furniture. Nothing extraneous should be placed on the table.
- In some Baptist churches, the two large chairs on either side of the Communion table are not for regular use.

- Stand when the Scriptures are being read before the sermon. There should be no talking or walking while the lesson is being read.
- No ministry group should meet without a period of devotion, e.g., prayer, Scripture reading, and a song.
- No walking during the Invitation to Christian Discipleship.
- When the pastor is absent, the presiding minister or guest minister is expected to carry out the service as if the pastor were there. There should be no changes from the standard order of service unless pre-approved by the pastor.
- If you are an assistant or an associate minister, under the leadership of a senior pastor, in the event that you have to be absent on a Sunday or for any occasion when your presence would normally be expected, you should notify the pastor or someone on the pastoral staff that you will not be present, and when you are expected to return.
- In churches with designated parking spaces, no one is permitted to park in the pastor's assigned space or the pastor's spouse's space.
- Ministers and deacons are expected to serve communion wearing white gloves.
- The Bible is not to be placed on the floor.
- No gum chewing in church.
- No eating or drinking in the sanctuary.
- Address older persons with a title, e.g. Mr. or Mrs.; Brother or Sister; Mother X or Deacon Y.
- Obey the ushers' direction.
- Do not throw trash on the grounds of the church.
- Do not make your own change during the distribution of the offering trays.

Remembering these protocols reminded me of a protocol expressed in a guest pastor's preliminaries. Astute observation of well-articulated preliminaries reveals a basic outline. The length of the preliminaries is designed to show the guest pastor's respect for his or her friend who issued the gracious invitation. The basic outline is as follows:

- Giving honor, first, to God, and then to a list of persons, beginning with the pastor, other ministers in the pulpit, officers, staff, members, and friends.

- Expressing thanks to God for being at the church.
- Acknowledging the hospitality that has been shown from the office staff and/or the driver, if not the pastor, who picked them up at the airport.
- Reviewing highlights of the trip to the city (if the guest is from another city or state).
- Introducing any guests that he or she may have brought with them. Some pastors travel with one or two armor-bearers.
- Expressing detailed appreciation for the pastor, which may include the following: history of their friendship, citing particular instances; may include a joke about their friendship; a word of praise for the church as a whole, usually called "a great church"; offering encouragement to the congregation to support their pastor.
- A closing statement of thanksgiving to God.

Wise Sayings

The wisdom of the elders was generously shared. Their wise sayings or proverbs were short, thereby making them memorable. Below is a collection of sayings that were frequently and freely offered by the elders at Pine Bluff Baptist Church.

- Never laugh or make fun of a handicapped person.
- Treat others the way you want to be treated.
- What's done in the dark will come to the light.
- Every tub has to sit on its own bottom.
- The person you mistreat on your way up, you may meet on your way down.
- You can't dig a ditch for someone else without getting in the ditch yourself.
- God helps those who help themselves.
- Don't leave worship like you came.
- God may not come when you want him to but he is always on time.
- Man changes; God never changes.
- God is no shorter than his word.
- Some people are better by nature than they are by practice.

- Get knowledge in your head; nobody can take it from you.
- God has given you a gift. If you don't use it, you will lose it.
- A person can have a college degree and still be an educated fool.
- Don't be so busy making a living that you don't make a life.
- Money ain't everything.
- Sister Lettie McCowan often quoted a popular saying: "There's some good in the worst of us; some bad in the best of us. It never behooves any of us to talk about the rest of us."
- If you make one step in faith, God will make two.
- Tomorrow is not promised to us. There is no time like today.
- I don't eat everybody's cooking.
- An empty wagon makes a lot of noise.
- Nothing worth having comes easy.
- Don't rest on your laurels. The work is not done.

Chapter Two

THE LORD'S SUPPER OR "CIRCAMENT" SUNDAY

Overview

Pine Bluff Baptist Church was well-attended on First Sundays. This was the day that the church gathered to remember the Lord's death by eating the bread and drinking the wine—symbols of Christ's body. A distinction in the manner of blessing and distributing the holy elements was the way in which the Communion covering was held up on each end by the deacons, as the pastor blessed the elements and the ushers distributed them to the members. This practice was done every First Sunday without fanfare. It merged effortlessly into the order of the Service.

When I began to examine this practice, I discovered that there were no written theological essays or popular reflections on it. When I asked around about its origin and meaning, I also discovered that very few church members and pastors had thought about its historical and theological roots. My sense is that contemporary explanations are secondary reflections while the primary origin and meanings have been lost. Nevertheless, I feel a compulsion to try to recover possible meanings and origin by covering as many possibilities as I can think of. The suggestions I put forward are not definitive; they are starting points for further conversation on this distinctive practice at the Lord's Table.

Dr. Zan Wesley Holmes, Jr., pastor emeritus of St. Luke "Community" United Methodist Church in Dallas, Texas, tells the story of a woman cooking a ham. One day her daughter asked her why she cut off the ends of the ham bone. Moved by her daughter's question, the mother asked her mother, and she replied: "I don't know. I've always cut the ends off the ham because that's what my grandmother always did." So, the two women decided to ask the great-grandmother if she knew why she, too, cut off the ends of the ham bone. She replied: "Because I didn't have a pan large enough."

Many times we don't know why we do what we do. However, this story also tells us that there is a reason why we do what we do. We have to be curious and diligent enough to search for the answer.

There's more to our history than has been remembered. There is truth in the maxim: The half has never been told. Unfortunately, many people act as if the present is all that matters. It is one thing to miss a piece of our story; it is another not to care that what's missing can help make us whole. Historical memory is related to the spiritual life. Dismissal of key social memories may not seem like much in a season of success, but success itself is hollow if it is not connected to a living past.

A favorite biblical story that addresses this insight is the story of Joshua and the People of Israel crossing the Jordan River. Joshua 4:1-7 states:

> When the entire nation had finished crossing over the Jordan, the Lord said to Joshua: "Select twelve men from the people, one from each tribe, and command them, 'Take twelve stones from here out of the middle of the Jordan, from the place where the priests' feet stood, carry them over with you, and lay them down in the place where you camp tonight.' "Then Joshua summoned the twelve men from the Israelites, whom he had appointed, one from each tribe. Joshua said to them, "Pass on before the ark of the Lord your God into the middle of the Jordan, and each of you take up a stone on his shoulder, one for each of the tribes of the Israelites, so that this may be a sign among you. When your children ask in time to come, 'What do those stones mean to you?' then you shall tell them that the waters of the Jordan were cut off in front of the ark of the covenant of the Lord. When it crossed over the Jordan, the waters of the Jordan were cut off. So, these stones shall be to the Israelites a memorial forever.

The beauty of this story is that each generation could witness the stones that were set up at Gilgal. Moreover, the interpretation of the meaning of the stones was not lost in the people's memory. When this story is read in light of the particular Black Baptist Communion practice, it is true to say that we have the material witness but have lost the sacred meaning of it.

This section of the book seeks to address the issue of the meaning of a particular Black Baptist Communion practice. That practice centers on the act of the deacons holding up the Communion covering—a white tablecloth—in front of the table while the minister prepares to give the bread and wine to the deacons for distribution to the congregation. What are the social and theological meanings of this practice?

I have searched for an answer in Black religious scholarship. It is not addressed in Melva Costen's classic text *African American Christian Worship*. It is not addressed in William McClain's insightful and personal essay on communion entitled "The Importance of Holy Communion: The African American Church and the Circament." It is not addressed by C. Eric Lincoln and Lawrence Mamiya in their monumental tome entitled *The Black Church in the African American Experience*. It is not addressed in the refreshing text, *Black Church Studies: An Introduction* edited by Stacey Floyd-Thomas, et al. It's not acknowledged by the Black Baptist educator Jesse Jai McNeil in *Minister's Service Book For Pulpit and Parish.*

The silence of Black religious scholars is no indication of the insignificance of this particular practice among some Black Baptists. Although the literature is silent, the Church still speaks as reflected in the continued existence of this practice. If the Church still speaks, then, every practice or ritual of the Black Church is potentially the subject of theological reflection by scholars, laity, and clergy.

My study of Black Church art as rendered by Black artists reveals a surprising oversight. There is a noticeable absence of this particular Communion practice in Black cultural art. Most artistic depictions of Black Church worship scenes focus on baptism, preaching, women shouting, choirs, church buildings, people entering the church, women in church hats, and people praying. A painting entitled "First Sunday" by Hulis Mavruk shows a woman and a young man holding up a little girl's hands. All three are dressed in white. The photo album-book, *Soul Sanctuary*, has some beautiful real-time photographs of Black people in church, but even this wonderful collection does not contain photographic versions of deacons holding up the Communion tablecloth during the observance of the Lord's Supper.

This presentation is an attempt to put this Black Baptist Church Communion practice into the community of dialogue, so that together, a responsible and realistic response may be given to the demanding question of its meaning or significance. In the absence of empirical evidence for the social origin of this practice, I began to ponder several hypotheses. I present them here in order to show the progression of my reflections and research on the practice in question.

I began my reflections and research with the following questions: What is the meaning of the act of the deacons holding up the white Communion tablecloth? What is its social origin? How could this practice still exist in some Black Baptist churches, and few lay members or pastors can explain its social, cultural, or theological meaning? Where are the churches that are known to have participated in this practice at some point in their history, or churches that currently engage this practice?

In conversations with several pastors and laypeople about this practice, I learned that the churches listed below either currently participate in this practice or did so at one point in their history:

- Pine Bluff Baptist Church in Karnack, Texas
- St. John Baptist Church in Marshall, Texas
- Concord Baptist Church in Dallas, Texas
- New Friendship Baptist Church in Dallas, Texas
- Greater New Zion Baptist Church in Dallas, Texas
- New Birth Baptist Church in Dallas, Texas
- True Lee Baptist Church in Dallas, Texas
- Good Street Baptist Church in Dallas, Texas
- St. Stephen Community Baptist Church in DeSoto, Texas
- Little Mount Zion Missionary Baptist Church in Brookshire, Texas
- Mount Pleasant Baptist Church in Houston, Texas
- Lilly Grove Baptist Church in Houston, Texas
- Orange Hill Baptist Church in Star, Louisiana

- Greater Travelers Rest Baptist Church in Atlanta, Georgia
- St. John Baptist Church in Oklahoma City, Oklahoma
- Union Progressive Baptist Church in Memphis, Tennessee
- Pleasant Green Baptist Church in Memphis, Tennessee
- Greater Olivet Baptist Church in Los Angeles, California
- Pleasant View Baptist Church in Birmingham, Alabama
- Mount Calvary Baptist Church in Leeds, Alabama
- Spring Hill Baptist Church in Tupelo, Mississippi
- New Providence Baptist Church in Tupelo, Mississippi
- White Hill Baptist Church in Tupelo, Mississippi
- Pine Grove Baptist Church in Shannon, Mississippi.

Some churches that used to engage in this practice stopped when the decision was made to use pre-packaged communion elements.

The first named church—Pine Bluff Baptist Church—is the congregation in which I was baptized, acknowledged my call to ministry, and first observed the practice of the deacons holding up the white Communion tablecloth. During my childhood, the Pine Bluff Baptist Church was led by Reverend J. H. Neely, and later by Reverend Joseph S. Cooper; the church met for worship on the first and third Sundays. Rev. Cooper also led the Mount Nebo Baptist Church in Vivian, Louisiana. It is likely that this same practice was done at the Mount Nebo Church.

I recall that after Reverend Cooper had preached and the invitation to Christian discipleship extended, he would transition to the Communion table. Sometimes he would stay in the pulpit and recite the events leading up to Jesus offering the bread and wine to His disciples. At the Communion table, he would call the deacons forward to assist in the distribution of the elements. Standing behind the table, he would continue to emphasize the spiritual significance of this occasion. Without fail he would remind the church of Paul's injunction not to eat and drink unworthily. Each of us was invited to take inventory of our lives and ask God's forgiveness. Then Deacon Wright would pray over the bread and Deacon Fitzpatrick would pray over the wine. Pastor Cooper would then recite the Words of Institution which consecrated the elements in remembrance of Jesus. The deacons would then hold up the corners of the white Communion sheet so as to shield the table from the congregation. Pastor Cooper would break the square-shaped unleavened bread, the cups having already been prepared by the Communion stewardesses. Trays of bread and cup would be distributed to all baptized church members. During the entire process, the chosen deacons continued to hold up the tablecloth until the Communion service ended with the church singing "I Know it was the Blood" or "There is a Fountain."

At each First Sunday observance of the Lord's Supper, both the bread and the wine were explained in light of Jesus' words at the Last Supper. At no time was the significance of the deacons holding up the Communion sheet explained to the congregation. Perhaps, for the older generation, having grown up with this practice, there was no need to explain since it was apparently understood. The problem is that the content of that self-understanding was not transmitted in teachable form to each succeeding generation. This was not a practice whose meaning could be grasped by osmosis or monthly repetition. It demanded sustained interpretation that has gone missing for decades.

To be sure that this practice was essentially limited to Black Baptists, I corresponded with several religion professors at East Texas Baptist University in Marshall, Texas. If this practice was "borrowed" from White Baptists in the larger Marshall area, there perhaps might remain persons who remembered the practice in White Baptist churches.

None of their comments indicated familiarity with the practice in question. Their comments lend some credence to the perspective that the practice in question was ingeniously designed by Black Christian Baptists to serve their spiritual needs. Unlike hymns, doctrines, polity, and the Church Covenant that were associated with White churches or more specifically with the Southern Baptist Church, this particular practice was not borrowed from White Southern Baptist churches.

Hypotheses

I turn now to some hypotheses that I formulated in my quest to answer questions about the origin and significance of the act of the deacons holding up the white Communion tablecloth while the minister breaks the bread and prepares the holy meal for distribution to the congregation.

As hypotheses, they may be connected to a concrete social circumstance or they may be unrealistic hunches. Either way, they provided starting points along a progression that would lead finally to some indigenous insights from elders in the church.

Internalized Racism?

My first hypothesis came to me while sitting in the pew on a Communion Sunday at a Black Baptist Church in Dallas. When I raised my head to see what was going on at the Communion table, to my great surprise, the deacons were holding up a white sheet in front of the table. Just as the overhead PowerPoint screen was showing various announcements, accompanied with visuals, I looked up and saw an Aryan portrayal of Jesus on the screen. My mind began to ponder the two scenes: the deacons holding up the white Communion tablecloth and a split-second portrayal of a white Jesus on the screen. Questions began to form in my mind. Was the Communion sheet functioning as a curtain to hide the holy elements from enslaved Black persons? Was this a practice used by Whites to keep enslaved Blacks from viewing the holy chalice and bread? Could this practice in Black Baptist churches be called internalized racism? If the white Communion sheet functions as a curtain to separate the good White communicants from enslaved Blacks, then is there a correlation with actual partitions in churches attended by both Whites and Blacks? It is well-documented that enslaved Blacks who attended church with their owners sat behind a wooden partition. In practical terms, at least in White churches that supported slavery, the sacrament of the Lord's Supper did not break down the dividing partition.

One can only wonder what enslaved Africans who had heard the gospel were thinking while sitting behind the dividing wall of physical and social segregation. How did they resolve this contradiction? Was it internalized? Did they reject it outright as an offense to the religion of Jesus?

The hypothesis that the act of the deacons holding up the white Communion tablecloth is an expression of internalized racism cannot be substantiated. The study of the existence of partitions in churches with mixed membership, while interesting, does not have a connection with the holding up of the white Communion sheet as a partition.

Late-Arriving Preacher?

My next hypothesis is that the act of holding up the white Communion tablecloth is connected with the late-arriving circuit preachers or pastors of multi-point churches. In the Marshall-Karnack, Texas area where I first witnessed this practice, many rural church pastors not only had two or more churches, they frequently changed pastorates. A reading of *A Brief History of Texas and Louisiana Baptist Association,* published in 1914, confirms, for example, that my home church, Pine Bluff Baptist Church, organized in 1869, had a string of pastors before Reverend Neely provided pastoral stability in the 1950s. Many rural churches met twice a month, e.g., first and third Sundays. A rural pastor of two or more churches was bound, at some point, given both weather and road conditions, to be late in arriving. The old Stagecoach Road being an unpaved thoroughfare must have delayed wagon and horse travel on rain-soaked days. On the Sundays when Holy Communion was served, it is plausible that the deacons and the congregation held prayer service, praise singing, and testimonies, up to the time the pastor arrived. It is also plausible that a late-arriving pastor would not have had the opportunity to gather with the deacons and/or deaconesses before the service to break the bread and pray with them over the holy elements. As a practical compensatory measure for a late-arriving pastor, then, when it came time to consecrate the elements, the deacons held up the white Communion tablecloth to provide a symbol of holy privacy for the breaking of the bread.

The following questions are raised by this hypothesis:

How did such a practice become so wide-spread, assuming that not every church responded in the same way to a late-arriving pastor?

Did Black Baptist pastors at the end of the nineteenth century and into the twentieth century meet with the deacons and/or Communion preparers before the worship service started in order to break the bread and bless the elements?

Did Black Baptist churches that participated in this practice wait on the pastor to arrive before starting worship service or was the service begun by deacons and others before the pastor arrived?

In the tradition of Black Baptists, the bread and wine are prepared privately by Communion Stewardesses. The pastor is not generally a participant during the preparation process. Because this was held to be a sacred meal, the preparation of it was not attended or observed by the general church public.

Veil in the Temple?

My next hypothesis is that the Communion practice is a portrayal of the veil in the Temple. This idea was suggested by several persons to whom I posed the question about the meaning of the white sheet being held up during the observance of the Lord's Supper.

In the Old Testament there are references to the inner sanctuary of the tabernacle or temple, also called the Holy of Holies. This inner space contained the Ark of the Covenant which held the Ten Commandments given to Moses on Mount Sinai. Only the High Priest could enter the inner sanctuary of the tabernacle or temple, and he did so only on the Day of Atonement. The Holy of Holies was separated from the rest of the tabernacle or temple by a veil. When the High Priest went behind the veil, he went to make atonement for himself and his household and the sins of the people, as described and prescribed in Leviticus 16.

In the New Testament, the gospels of Matthew, Mark, and Luke state that upon the death of Jesus "the curtain of the temple was torn in two" (Matthew 27:51; Mark 15:38; and Luke 23:45).

In chapter 9 of the Book of Hebrews, the writer acknowledges the Day of Atonement and the work of the High Priest in the inner sanctuary. The writer of Hebrews points out that this sacrifice had to be carried out in detail every year without fail. As if possessed by an explosive insight, the writer states:

But when Christ came as a high priest of the good things that have come, then through the greater and perfect tent (not made with hands, that is, not of this creation), he entered once for all into the Holy Place, not with the blood of goats and calves, but with his own blood, thus obtaining eternal redemption. For if the blood of goats and bulls, with the sprinkling of the ashes of a heifer, sanctified those who have been defiled so that their flesh is purified, how much more will the blood of Christ, who through the eternal Spirit offered himself without blemish to

God, purify our conscience from dead works to worship the living God! (Hebrews 9:11-14).

When these three Scriptures (Leviticus 16; Matthew 27:51; and Hebrews 9) were prayerfully pondered and preached by Black preachers and their congregations, I wonder if there leaped into the Black worshiping imagination the act of holding up the white Communion tablecloth as an emblem of the curtain that Christ entered to effect salvation for all through his death on the cross. The image of the veil being split in two is a consideration; however, one has to remember that, according to one gospel account, the veil was split. The Communion tablecloth is never presented torn or ripped.

A Health-Related Measure?

My next hypothesis is that the practice in question is related to a national health crisis. In 1904 the National Association for the Study and Prevention of Tuberculosis was formed to address the dreaded disease called consumption. The initial emphasis was on hygiene. This disease was racialized as "the White Plague" because the White community was led to believe that its own health was in dire jeopardy from Blacks who worked in and around their homes and businesses. It had been established by the Surgeon General's office that tuberculosis or consumption affected Black people three times the rate of Whites. While the "White Plague" notion was rooted in negative portrayals of Blacks as carriers of disease and filth, little attention was given to the social conditions that Black people had to endure, in both rural settings and city dwellings. Instead of addressing the systemic social causes of Black people's poor health, the White community made their maids and porters the pariahs who trafficked in all sorts of diseases. Many Black leaders, including W. E. B. DuBois, Willis J. King, Kelly Miller, and Lugenia Burns Hope, called attention to unsanitary conditions in which Black people were forced to live.

Although the National Association for the Study and Prevention of Tuberculosis published literature on how to prevent the spread of the disease, the Black community did not become a national focus for dealing with tuberculosis until the Surgeon General's office appointed Dr. Charles P. Wertenbaker, a surgeon, to develop a plan for organizing

Blacks to combat the disease. Dr. Wertenbaker's Plan had the ambitious goal of establishing an anti-tuberculosis league in every Black church. In Louisiana the Colored Anti-tuberculosis League, led by Dr. J. H. Murray of Patterson, Louisiana, was organized in 1909. The measures to combat this disease included: wiping all appliances, vacuuming or cleaning away every particle of dust, keeping flies out of the home, using a handkerchief or tissue to cover one's cough, and using a cup or a spittoon to collect spit. Cleaning measures were particularly emphasized in churches that freely engaged in shouting or exuberant praise.

The mention of spitting and shouting in churches led to the hypothesis that the practice in question may have been created as a health measure. This hypothesis is plausible in small rural churches in which there wasn't a lot of space between the front pews and the Communion table.

As is still the case today, ministers were called upon to assist in educating the Black community about the disease and ways to combat it. As a public venue, churches had to be concerned since the weekly or bi-monthly gathering was susceptible to the spread of the disease. Moreover, Communion Sunday, the highest attended Sunday of the month, would be of utmost concern in the minds of those combating tuberculosis.

It is reasonable to assume that there had to be concern for the care of the Communion elements. A white cloth was placed over the elements to prevent flies from settling on the cup and bread. Perhaps instructors of the anti-tuberculosis campaign said enough for ministers to take the next step in signaling their concern for the spread of the disease by having the Communion covering raised during the distribution of the elements so that moisture from sneezing, coughing, spitting, and sweating would not contaminate the cup and the bread.

This hypothesis raises the following questions:

Since a national conversation was birthed on whether to keep the common cup or use individual communion cups, did Black church leaders take a public stand on this debate? When did Black Baptists change from a common cup to individual cups for Holy Communion?

Did the practice of holding up the Communion sheet come into vogue in some churches about the same time that individual trays of small cups were decided upon?

In a conversation with my niece, Faye Hall, who at the time was an octogenarian—believe it or not—she shared a memory that on First Sundays the St. John Baptist Church in Marshall used a common cup. This was in 1940, under the pastoral leadership of Reverend J. R. Rutledge. My niece, being a young girl at the age of eleven, was captivated by the shine on the silver goblet as it was passed in the pews. After each member took a sip from the cup, it was wiped with a white cloth.

A Dramatic Re-enactment?

My next hypothesis is that the act of the deacons holding up the white Communion tablecloth is part of the drama or re-enactment of the Lord's Supper.

Worship in the traditional Black Baptist church was filled with dramatic scenes, including: deacons intoning the classic African-American prayer; the congregation humming or moaning during all the prayers; the choir processing down the center aisle with orchestrated movement as members sang and clapped and swayed their way to the choir stand; signaling ushers who practiced precision in their nonverbal display of importance; preachers who stand as the late-entering pastor or guest preacher enters the pulpit; the musical whooping of the preacher; the white-gloved deacons dressed to the nines with coordinated ties and Black suits; the first lady being escorted to her seat with grace and dignity, as all eyes take pride in her classy outfit.

Accompanying these dramatic scenes on the First Sunday in a traditional Black Baptist church is the dramatic visual display of Jesus with his disciples in the Upper Room. This hypothesis asserts that the raised sheet is a prop in the drama of rehearsing Jesus' words and actions in that Last Supper scene. Just as the verses of hymns were lined to accommodate formerly enslaved persons who could not read, the drama hypothesis assumes a growing literacy among mostly rural Black Baptists. The whole scene of the pastor standing at the Communion table, surrounded by deacons, and the tablecloth being held up, is an image of the Last Supper. The drama helped those who could not read to enter into the story of the Last Supper. The pastor would tell the story of Jesus at the table as recorded in the gospels. He would recite the words of Jesus: "Do this in remembrance of me" or "I will drink no more of the fruit of the vine until I drink it new with you in my Father's kingdom."

Perhaps the raised Communion sheet points away from itself to the main dialogue or the main meal in the drama of the Last Supper. Like props in a stage play or tablecloths on a dinner table, the sheet participates but does not dominate the narrative of the Last Supper.

This act should remind us of the creative imagination of our ancestors who accented the ordinance of the Lord's Supper by holding up the Communion sheet. Each time this act is performed it keeps alive a cultural link with a past that continues to teach us about creativity, resilience, and the power of theological imagination.

Beyond the holding up of the crisp white Communion tablecloth and beyond the white gloves adorning the deacons' hands, is a vital, vibrant, story of God's love toward us. On any given Communion Sunday in Black Baptist churches, one hears the congregation singing:

"I Know it was the Blood."

"There is a Fountain Filled with Blood."

"Let Us Break Bread Together on Our Knees."

The Lord's Supper, with all of its accompanying movements, is about the width, the depth, the breadth, and the height of God's love.

This hypothesis leads to the following question: In the early part of the twentieth century, was there a dramatic play or skit performed at the National Baptist Convention or National Congress or at the Women's Convention, that so captured the audience that pastors were inspired and encouraged to add this practice to the observance of the Lord's Supper?

At-Home Deaths?

My next hypothesis regarding the act of the deacons holding up the white Communion sheet has to do with at-home deaths in the early part of the twentieth century. My hypothesis is that there is a connection between the raising of the white sheet at the Communion table and a sheet being held up in the process of attending to at-home deaths. In pursuit of this hypothesis, I sent the following letter to several funeral home directors and to a couple of mortuary science instructors:

> *I write to invite your thoughts on a research question for a project on which I am working. My question has to do with an early twentieth century practice of preparing the deceased's body in the home. I have read several Internet sites that confirm that the body of the deceased was washed and dressed sometimes by family members before the embalmer arrived. I want to know if in rural Black communities in the South, where the water source and the tub were outside, was a sheet or a covering used to preserve the dignity of the body while it was being washed. For example, after the death, would there not be children and neighbors coming by; so, did the family members or others who did the washing and dressing, maybe outside the house, use a sheet to keep others from viewing the body? How was the dignity of the deceased preserved during the entire process if the preparation was done at home with a cooling board?*

Responses from a couple of morticians confirmed that a white sheet was used in earlier times to protect the modesty of the body during preparation, and that the body was washed and dressed at home by women. The body of the deceased was laid on a cooling board. This is the historic basis of the expression in the classic deacon's prayer: "Lord, we thank you that our bed was not our cooling board."

It is a common practice to use a sheet at death to preserve the dignity of the body. The common elements in this hypothesis are the body of the decedent and a white sheet. It is plausible that the deacons raised the white Communion sheet to preserve the dignity of the body of Jesus while the pastor prepared the body (bread and wine).

In August 1955, the world witnessed the power of what a lowered sheet can reveal. A young boy named Emmett Till was visiting relatives in Money, Mississippi, when he reportedly whistled at a White woman in a convenience store. The report of this incident infuriated two White men, who grabbed Emmett from his home, beat him, wrapped his innocent body in barbed wire, and threw him in the Tallahatchie River.

His mother, Mamie Till, finally yielded to the wisdom of those who counseled her to leave his body in an open casket. The world was shocked when the proverbial sheet was removed to reveal the brutality of White racism.

Likewise, at the Communion table, the tablecloth, when covering the elements as well as when it is held up, is preserving the dignity and holiness of the body of Jesus. But when it is removed from the bread (the body of Jesus), the Church beholds the brutality of hatred against Jesus, the Chosen One of God. The sheet records both the holiness of the body of Jesus and the meanness of the world toward him.

O if the Communion sheet could talk! On the one hand, the sheet would talk about the dignity, the holiness of Jesus. He was conceived by the Holy Spirit. He came to help his people, but they rejected him. He helped the helpless; offered living water to thirsty souls; honored the poor with the good news of God being with them. He wanted the house of God to be respected as a holy place and its leaders to treat the poor with holy dignity.

On the other hand, the sheet would talk about the hatred and meanness imposed on Jesus. He was accused of getting his power from the devil. He was perceived to be crazy. He was betrayed by Judas; endured the humiliation of a kangaroo court. He was spat on, slapped, mocked, and nailed to a Roman cross.

So, the Communion sheet is regaling the sacredness of the body of Jesus, and revealing the logic of human cruelty against God's Son.

African Motifs?

My next hypothesis comes from a suggestion made to me by Dr. Jeremiah A. Wright, Jr., pastor emeritus of the Trinity United Church of Christ in Chicago. After sharing his opinions about this practice, Dr. Wright recommended that I take another look at the work of Dr. Henry Mitchell in his classic text *Black Belief.*

In *Black Belief,* Mitchell stands in solidarity with scholars like Melville Herskovits and W.E.B. Du Bois who researched the connections in African-American culture with African ways of being. In several studies these proposed connections are referred to as "Africanisms" or retentions of African culture. Unlike E. Franklin Frazier in his classic study, *The Negro Church in America,* Mitchell and Herskovits assert that the African belief system did not die in the furnace of European-American slavery but survived, for example, in language, music, and Spirit-possession.

Scholars like Mitchell, Herskovits, and Du Bois are seeking to correct the notion of dismissing or overlooking the African world view in favor of the European Christian ideals. Many religious insights or expressions designed by Africans were not judged to be theirs but must have a European origin. This is the legacy of miseducation that Carter G. Woodson addresses in his classic text *The Miseducation of the Negro.* It is true that some Black southern Christians, in an effort to imbibe the thoughts and ways of the White academy and society at large, looked askance at certain practices and beliefs of their elders. These old ways and beliefs were considered "old fogey"—a way of judging certain African distinctions as inappropriate or irrelevant for an enlightened era. Moaning during prayers, humming, lining hymns, and holding up the white Communion tablecloth, perhaps lost some relevance to a post-Civil Rights generation and to the succeeding generation shaped in a highly mobile, technological society. The rush to update our socio-economic image risked leaving behind the spiritual or theological understandings which supported these earlier expressions of Black faith. Underneath this judgment lies a moral and spiritual network of negotiating life's adversities that we would do well to unearth and re-think for our own spiritual and moral good.

Taking the rich insights of African cultural retentions into consideration, the act of holding up the white Communion sheet may be assumed to have a connection with a deep African belief. While it is not possible to date the origin of this practice, Mitchell's work suggests that we can come to some important insights about the cultural source and meaning of it. The African influence that may reside in this practice suggests something about the priest or clergy who had to have the spiritual knowledge and cultural sensitivity to handle the sacred elements. Not unlike the expectations today that priests or clergy need to have authority and knowledge to preach or preside at the table or baptize, there is a deep expectation stemming from African culture that the priests know what elements to use, how to use them, and what words to use with them, to affect the desired outcomes, e.g., healing or reconciliation or an encounter with unseen realities.

Moreover, as Black pastors and congregations creatively altered the received white Protestant Baptist liturgy to fit their own needs, the alteration itself was authored by the prevenient presence of African cultural wisdom. The main elements of the Communion service in traditional Baptist churches were bread and cup, but the African cultural genius moved in the collective hearts and minds of pastors and churches to add the act of holding up the white Communion tablecloth—not simply as an aesthetic addition, but to heighten the presence of the Divine in the midst of the gathered community. The service at the table included prayers, homilies, the Words of Institution, the breaking of the bread and the passing of the cup, but the raising of the table covering in Black Baptist churches took on an importance commensurate with the bread and cup. In other words, Communion included the bread, the cup, and the white sheet. In order for the mysterious power of God to be experienced, not only must there be unleavened bread and grape juice (symbolic of the blood of Jesus), but a white tablecloth, carefully washed, lovingly ironed, prayerfully brought to the church, reverently placed on the table, and at the actual service of Communion, that same tablecloth is ritually held up as one of the mediums for the people to encounter the presence of the Holy in the midst of their humanity, redeemed by the sacrificial act of Jesus.

Could it be that resident in the deep cellular chambers of African memory in America, there is a spiritual meaning and power mediated by the raised Communion cloth? In the act of holding up the white Communion tablecloth there may be a faint remembrance of communion and fellowship with our ancestors through pouring libations or offering food to them. Moreover, the white Communion sheet becomes a symbol that God desires to be in communion with us by piercing the veil and overcoming every obstacle to our communion with God. Each time that we participate in the African-oriented ritual of eating the bread and drinking the wine, we enter into a living communion with Jesus who was dead but is alive through our remembrance of him in the community of faith.

An African belief that may assist us here is the idea that symbols have power; they can be invested with the energy to link persons with their ancestors and with God. A symbol can be in nature, such as a tree, a rock, or a stream, or made by humans; symbols can be special people, words, signs, gestures, or material fabrics. It is by God's power that the common becomes extraordinary, and can be employed to participate in ministries of healing or revoking evil powers. The creative breath of God is alive and is still making it possible for inanimate objects to be used as potential vessels in connecting the sacred and the secular. Moreover, based on the image of God in human beings, persons may decide in community that certain objects or people may be incorporated into the sacred realm of power. It used to be a common belief among African Americans that a child born with a veil over her face had a special gift or calling. The power that a special object or person may hold does not come into the ordinary realm for use until there is a belief in the community that such an element or person can serve as a vital link with a source of mystery or higher power. Believing that power is resident in such a thing or person makes it possible for the believer to share in the blessing that is gifted in a particular artifact, thing, or person. As such, the white Communion tablecloth, in the context of African symbolism, was raised by our ancestors as a conduit of divine energy, and the acceptance of it by the community validated its power to add sacred meaning to the Communion ritual.

This hypothesis raises the following question: How can we account for the wide-spread use of this practice in states such as Texas, Louisiana, Mississippi, Alabama, Tennessee, Oklahoma, and Georgia? My response is that it may be accounted for not by a fiat from the office of the president of the National Baptist Convention, but is rather a clear expression of African cultural unity. No one had to send a memo to all these participating churches asking for cooperation in this prescribed ritual. The practice itself is an illustration of the power of this deeply-rooted African spirit seeking unity or commonality in the worship life of an oppressed Black people. As people migrated from the south to the north, so did their belief systems and cultural practices. When the migration theory is contemplated in light of the Communion practice, the following views can be posited regarding the African presence underlying that practice:

1. Life continues after death.
2. Africans are careful to maintain good horizontal and vertical relationships.

3. Ancestors live in the community's memory.
4. Ancestors and spirits mediate blessings and prayer requests.
5. Food and drink are portions of honoring the ancestors.
6. The color white is widely associated with death.
7. Counter-clockwise movement, e.g., the ring shout expresses a spiritual transformation of consciousness.

These, and many other views, are at the core of the Communion practice.

At Pine Bluff Baptist Church, after everyone was served bread and wine, and the minister offered closing remarks, every member walked around in a circle, moving in a counter-clockwise orientation, shaking hands with the pastor, deacons, and every member. Reminiscent of the circle associated with the sacred ring shout, the counter-clockwise movement of shaking hands or giving the right hand of fellowship, was a way of inviting the Spirit to maintain the social and spiritual unity begun in the worship experience and summed up in the taking of the Lord's Supper. While shouting took place during the traditional Baptist worship experience, the sacred ring, formed only after taking the Lord's Supper, held the African values of community, fellowship, and love for one another and God. Symbolically, the members were participating in the African movement of life—from birth, to growth, to maturity in wisdom, and to unity with the ancestors and God in rebirth. This creative movement in consciousness has a tri-center-- communion with God, one another, and the fruit of the earth.

In the community of Pine Bluff Baptist Church, the Lord's Supper was also called Circament. I often heard older church members express their excitement to go and get their Circament. Could this term be a combination of the words Circle and Sacrament? The sacrament referred to the elements of bread and wine, but the circle referred to the mysterious movement from birth to new life in the presence of the community and God. What sounds like a mispronunciation may contain a pronouncement that needs to be respected and honored.

Belief in Benevolent and Malevolent Spirits?

Our African ancestors brought with them a dynamic belief in the existence and power of spirits. There was a pantheon of spirits that had to be recognized, honored, or controlled through ceremonies and precise rituals. Spirits populated human communities expressed in disease, sickness, misfortune, as well as in the natural realm such as trees and rivers. Almost daily attention to the workings of these spirits was the work of medicine specialists and village priests. At the experience of deaths in the village, for example, family members were expected to engage in certain practices, lest the spirit of the deceased either return to speak or do harm.

Africans who were brought to these shores did not jettison their worldview concerning the workings of spirits. As they were introduced to Christianity, as is popularly acknowledged, they were not so much converted to Christianity as they converted the religion to meet their own ends. Although many Africans went through the motions of accepting the religion of their oppressors, they overlaid the religious views of their White teachers with their African understandings. Thus, they kept some beliefs concerning God, ancestors, and evil spirits.

There slowly emerged a set of superstitions that stood alongside Christian teachings. There were superstitions about walking between two trees, or coming to a crossroad, or seeing "haints" or spirits in the cemetery or covering clocks with Black cloth when someone died. Many Africans carried charms on their bodies as a way of warding off potential evil spirits. Objects that were invested with special powers included an animal part, or beads, or human hair or grave dirt.

As Africans began to establish their own churches, particularly Baptist churches, after 1865, many of these beliefs and superstitions were integral to daily life in community. The belief that the Spirit will not descend without a song played a major role in the worship life of the church. African ideas about malevolent spirits were summarized in the belief in the devil or Satan. Several of the Spirituals bear witness to the belief in the existence of the devil and his work. When the church gathered for worship in many southern, rural Black Baptist churches, there were dynamic beliefs in the sovereignty of God and in the presence and work of the devil. They gathered to praise the Creator-God with the recognition that the spirit of the devil was always trying to access human and spiritual resources for malevolent ends. One Spiritual talks about the devil aiming to catch our souls but missed and grabbed our sins, and went limping back to hell, mumbling his defeat. One song that is sung today says: "I woke up this morning with my mind stayed on Jesus. Hallelu. The devil can't get you with your mind stayed on Jesus." By baptism and conversion, the faithful are committed to Jesus but the devil still tries to lure committed believers away from the works of God. So the church engages in practices to glorify or manifest God's presence in worship. Obviously singing and praying and testifying are key practices to aid the manifestation of God's Spirit in the body of Christ.

Of the Sundays that the church gathers for worship, Black Baptists focused centrally on the first Sunday of the month for the observance of the Lord's Supper. Many churches held this observance at night. Our ancestors had some beliefs or superstitions about night or darkness. Spirits moved in and through the woods and cemeteries at night. Many churchgoers had to either walk or ride wagons or horses to get to the church at night for the Lord's Supper. Upon safely arriving to the church, they enthusiastically joined in acts of praise. The Lord's Supper at night enjoined the community to worship God in spirit and in truth, since malevolent spirits roved at night, in both the physical and spiritual parts of the world.

During the service of the Lord's Supper, the community sang and prayed as a way of inviting God's Spirit to possess the entire baptized congregation. The fervent songs and prayers warded off any destructive or hateful spirit that the devil intended to use to disrupt the purpose of the occasion. Central to the practice of observing the Lord's Supper was the act of the deacons raising the white Communion tablecloth while the minister broke the bread, while the wine, representing Jesus' blood, was already prepared. In the African belief system that I have presented, could the holding up of the white table cloth be a way of cordoning off the precinct around the table as truly holy, so that the devil or any evil spirit could not trespass? If the evil spirit was looking for a life-force such as the blood of Jesus to continue its community-disrupting work, then, it found the raised white sheet as a "no trespassing" symbol. In this interpretation, the raised white Communion sheet is not hiding the sacred elements from the congregants, but it is protecting the holiness of the table from the malevolent intentions of the evil one.

This interpretation explains, in part, why the meaning of the act of raising the white Communion sheet is lost in the memory of the practicing community of faith. The loss is connected with a worldview that includes superstitions or the existence of a pantheon of spirits. With formerly enslaved persons and their descendants having greater access to Western education, this practice and its meaning began to fade. Modernity, with its loyalty to science, questioned the role of the unseen in a thoroughly empirical world. In many churches the act continues while the meaning has been lost. It is sacred work to recover that meaning since the act does continue in many churches.

Coded Messages in Slavery and Jim Crow Era?

For further conversation I want to propose that another way of addressing the question of origin is not to look for dates but to acknowledge the living contexts in which this practice evolved. Beyond geographical context is the ideological and functional contexts of Jim Crowism. The era of Jim Crow (and Jane Crow) may largely be defined as that period from the end of Reconstruction (1877) to the rise of the modern Civil Rights Movement (mid-1950s). Within this temporal swath most traditional Black Baptist churches either matured or had their origin.

A look at Jim Crowism is important for this study because it defined the social, political, economic, and religious life of southern Blacks in the United States. More specifically, laws were enacted and customs reinforced that established the inferior status of Blacks in the minds of Whites who considered themselves naturally superior to Blacks. There were White democratic primaries that excluded Black political participation. There were laws against intermarriage. Blacks and Whites could not ride in the same coaches or compartments on public transportation. When the Supreme Court in 1883 struck down the Civil Rights Act of 1875, Blacks were disenfranchised from White restaurants, entertainment venues, and hotels. Blacks and Whites went to separate educational institutions. In 1896 the Supreme Court upheld the "separate but equal" doctrine in the landmark ruling known as *Plessy v. Ferguson*. In this same period

Black people had to survive in the face of discrimination in employment, housing, schooling, and military service.

Within the segregationist ideology, it was an *a priori* maxim that there would be White churches and Black churches. Strangely enough, Whites did not want Blacks attending their churches but Blacks were generally more disposed to expressing hospitality to Whites. Black preachers took seriously the "Whosoever will" spirit of openness in Christ's church. Also, Black Christians did not want to foreclose on the possibility that the visiting stranger might be an angel of God. These internalized spiritual claims made Black Christians more susceptible to welcoming Whites even though they were not welcome in White southern churches. It was not uncommon during the era of Jim Crow for traditional Black churches to reserve seats for Whites at church recitals, plays, or a city-wide campaign against a common foe, for example, tuberculosis or influenza.

The long arm of Jim Crow or the extended reach of White racism eventually found its way into Black religious life. Theological ideas about Black being equated with evil and White with good had to be deconstructed in holy spaces. The white picture of Jesus on the church walls or the image of God as a White man oppressed Black psyches.

While the tortured tentacles of White racism or Jim Crow dominated Black life, including Black religious life, I assert that there was a limit or a line that Black preachers and churches stood behind that could not be trespassed by the presence of Jim Crow.

To establish this assertion, I want to re-visit a practice that our ancestors in American slavery used to aid both their survival and liberation. That practice has been called using double-coded messages, studied mostly by interpreters of the Spirituals. Many of the spirituals had a religious message with a social meaning. The song "Everybody Talkin' 'Bout Heaven Ain't Going There" has been interpreted as a critique of church-going slave masters who mistreated enslaved persons. Songs about Canaan were interpreted as a message not only about heaven but about the North, Canada, where freedom resided. The popular song "We are Climbing Jacob's Ladder" could be interpreted as a code about progressing safely on the Underground Railroad—a collection of sites with abolitionists ready to send enslaved runaways to the next station on the long journey to freedom.

Another locus of the practice of coded signals is quilt-making. In *Hidden in Plain View*, Jacqueline Tobin and Raymond G. Dobard confirm that quilt codes were used visually to assist enslaved persons in their escape on the Underground Railroad. Coded messages in quilts provided information for preparation to learning which paths to take, the distance between safe sites, roads and landmarks, and how much farther to go to reach Canada or freedom. Everything on coded quilts had meaning, including the length and spacing of stitches and the number of knots or ties. In essence, ingenious quilt-makers used available information to design a virtual roadmap to freedom without arousing suspicion from White slave owners. I am asserting that another expression of this code-bearing practice of our ancestors is the raised Communion sheet. It, too, like the Spirituals and code-carrying quilts, is a co-participant in saying one thing but meaning something else.

In keeping with the claim that flies had to be kept off the Lord's Supper, the justice-denying atmosphere of Jim Crow and White racism provided the perfect birthing sac for the hatching of flies—not insects—but the flies of miseducation, self-hatred, low self-esteem, inferiority, internalized attitudes of Blacks as lazy and good-for-nothings. However, in the doubled-coded meaning of Black religious symbolism, these flies were thwarted by the white Communion covering on the bread and wine. The area of the Lord's Table was a no-fly zone for the flies and fleas that bore spirit-sapping and soul-destroying diseases. Black worshipers could be assured, as the Communion sheet was held up by the senior deacons, that they were partaking of the holy body of Jesus that had not been polluted by the inferiority-breeding diseases and discourses of White racism.

Could it be that the Black preacher at the Communion table functioned as the one responsible for not only shooing, swatting, fanning, flies off the bread and wine, but preventing the psychological and spiritual flies from lighting on the partakers of the holy elements? The held-up Communion sheet is integral to the shoo-fly message. The shoo-fly message is that oppressed Black Christians, living in an anti-Black society, have the spiritual authority to ban every hate-filled fly from the sanctuary and table of the Lord. In truth, through baptism and Communion, they belong to God, who gave his only Son to set them free in the service of liberation and justice. They don't belong to any slave master, landowner, corporate bank, or political party. Their ultimate identification is children of God who have been invited by Jesus to eat and drink of heaven's unbounded grace and love. The message is that at the Table of the Lord or in the Company of the Saints, they could say that they felt like a shining star, meaning that their full God-intended humanity has been restored and reclaimed. Anything not of God has to go, be shooed away; anything not affirming God's image in us has to be shooed away with the breath of new life and determination.

This presentation has established several perspectives along a spiritual or theological trajectory of meanings. The other side of this code-carrying Communion tablecloth is its defiant assertion that Jim Crow and white supremacy stop there. The sanctuary of the church might be peopled with persons carrying the marks, signs, scars, and burdens of oppressive Jim Crow, but there is a space within the peopled-sanctuary where the curled and crooked fingers of Jim and Jane Crow cannot reach or control. That space is symbolically marked by the raised Communion sheet.

Behind the raised Communion sheet lay bread and wine, elements used by Jesus in the Last Supper, which we interpret symbolically to mean the body and blood of the Lord Jesus. These elements also point to the horrible crucifixion of Jesus on the cross at Calvary. Both Jesus' communion with his disciples and the crucifixion of Jesus are fixed points in Black churches' understanding of the constellation of salvation and freedom. These are fixed points upon which the eyes of Black Christians are fixed as they both hear the story of salvation and prepare to partake of the body and blood of Jesus. Black Christians come to several positive affirmations about what is behind the raised Communion sheet. These affirmations include:

- That no earthly power can stop them from being in communion with God or stop God from being in communion with them;
- That as children of the Living God, they have a right to sit at the Welcome Table without fear of exclusionary racist laws;

- That they might be nobodies in the eyes of Jim Crow society but in the eyes of God they are whole human beings who are invited to the heavenly banquet;
- That their participation at the table means that Jesus identifies with their sufferings;
- That their bodies, though oppressed, matter with God, and they, therefore, can lift up their heads with dignity because God is their Heavenly Father;
- That the grace and mercies of God, expressed in Jesus' death for human redemption, never fails. Food may be scarce in other places, but the bread of heaven is forevermore and for everyone.

These are the inviolate affirmations that keep Black people coming back to the Table of the Lord every time the invitation is given. Black Christians come to the table rejoicing that the powers of this world have no authority over the distribution of divine grace and heaven-bought earthly freedom.

The Linen Cloth in the Tomb?

Since the question that I am pursuing has to do with the linen cloth covering the Communion table, I am positing the notion that African American Baptists of an earlier era reflected upon three texts as these relate to the creation of the practice of holding up the Communion cloth.

I believe that our ancestors knew the major stories in the Bible even if many of them could not read. They heard the preacher elaborate on the stories with great power and imagination. Intertwining the biblical stories in response to their own lived experiences was a mode of interpreting Scripture. Contemporary Bible scholars may refer to this as the method of intertextuality. Stories were connected to make sense of their own lives as well as to mark what they considered to be important messages in the Bible. In the context of the Communion cloth and the practice of holding it up before the audience, it is likely that as preachers, deacons and members read the Bible privately and in community, there emerged the idea of the raised Communion table cloth.

The first step that helped to shape this practice was the reading of Luke 24:12 and John 20:3-7. Luke 24:12 states, *But Peter got up and ran to the tomb; stooping and looking in, he saw the linen cloths by themselves; then he went home, amazed at what had happened.* John 20: 3-7 states, *Then Peter and the other disciple set out and went toward the tomb. The two were running together, but the other disciple out ran Peter and reached the tomb first. He bent down to look in and saw the linen wrappings lying there, but did not go in. Then Simon Peter came, following him, and went into the tomb. He saw the linen wrappings lying there....*

In Leviticus 18 is a list of prohibitions against seeing the nakedness of family members and others. In the community that established the practice of holding up the Communion sheet, covering was used out of respect for the body. Our ancestors knew that no one walks around naked. So how then did they respond to the resurrected Jesus whose linen cloths are left in the tomb?

The next step that helped to shape the practice of holding up the linen Communion cloth was to read the book of Revelation, particularly chapter 19. Rev. 19:7-8 states, *Let us rejoice and exult and give him glory, for the marriage of the Lamb has come, and his bride has made herself ready; to her it has been granted to be clothed with fine linen, bright and pure—for the fine linen is the righteous deeds of the saints.* The image of marriage is used to express the abiding unity between God and the Church. All the faithful saints are invited to the marriage supper (v.9), a reference to the messianic banquet symbolized in the Lord's Supper. Their steadfast commitment to Jesus is poetically spoken of as "fine linen." So the Church can anticipate at each observance of the Lord's Supper the blessing of being united forever in faith to God through Jesus. Our ancestors perceived the Communion linen cloth as a symbol of a future wherein they will forever be with the resurrected Jesus, who himself is clothed in splendid righteousness.

As they read further in Revelation 19, our ancestors discovered that the resurrected Jesus "*is clothed in a robe dipped in blood, and his name is called The Word of God*" (19:13). This is another symbolic reference to the blood Jesus shed for the redemption of those who put their faith in God. The linen cloth worn by Jesus is the same in his life and ministry as in his death, resurrection, and glorious reign. It is the same because it represents his faithfulness to God. The linen cloth left in the tomb is there to remind the Church that the faithful followers of Jesus will also be clothed in redemptive righteousness, both spiritual and social, if they take up their cross and follow Jesus.

Concluding Possibilities

It needs to be remembered that the act of holding up the white Communion sheet in traditional Black Baptist churches began in the era of Jim Crow. Blacks could not enter into White churches in the south to worship. The opposite, however, was that Whites could come into a Black church without being put out. Perhaps this ritual within the ritual of the Lord's Supper was generated by the context of Whites attending Black worship services. On Communion Sunday, perhaps just like in the general community, seats at Black-church sponsored events were often reserved for Whites. With Whites sitting on the front pew or close to the front, a minister with authority and influence in the Black Baptist denomination, decided that the deacons should hold up the white Communion covering as a ritual. Why? Perhaps to say to Whites in attendance that they do not control what goes on at the Lord's Table. Perhaps it was to say to Black folks that they must maintain not only their integrity as persons but the integrity of the table. The table was one place where the authority of White presence ended. The raised sheet was the limit of white power. Unknown to Whites in attendance, the Black minister and deacons were exercising Black power on behalf of both the sacredness of the holy meal and the sacredness of Black bodies. Whites may be seated on the front pew, but Black leaders determined what was viewed or not viewed. Holding the sheet up throughout the ritual asserted that at no time during the holy meal would the gaze of White folks compromise the righteousness of what God had done in Jesus Christ. In the context of Jim Crow, Whites saw themselves as superior to Blacks, which is why they could walk into any Black church without creating a fuss. Blacks accepted this insult without revolt. However, a quiet revolution took place at the Lord's Table when Black church leaders took charge of the meaning and manner in which the Supper would be handled. No one outside of the Black community could dictate the order of this service or the aesthetics that went along with it. This was Black church folks putting up a veil to shield the holy table from the eyes of those who did not allow these same Blacks to worship in their churches. Through this ritual Black preachers and deacons were retaining the power of the gospel to be used for human liberation void of every form of racial insult or injustice.

I imagine that the preacher would extol the congregation to remember the life, sufferings, and death of Jesus, often in vivid language. Concurrently, the Black preacher exhorted the members to remember their own sufferings, lashings, rapes, humiliations, and lynching of family members and friends. In this way, the Black Church was keeping alive an intimate connection with the sufferings and death of Jesus. However, when Whites were in the audience, the Black preacher may have switched to a homily at the table that focused on the awful treatment of Jesus at the hands of his torturers. Black worshipers knew what was going on. They were remembering their own story even as the preacher exhorted them to remember the death of Jesus. In this context, a practice was created that had deep roots in the old-time religion of enslaved Africans. That practice involved helping the church to drink the cup and eat the bread in memory of Jesus, but also hold up the white Communion covering at the same time.

Through this creative act, the words of Jesus had a double meaning. Jesus said, "Do this in remembrance of me." As the preacher quoted these words, he was also speaking on behalf of the gathered community to the next generation — "Do this in remembrance of me (us)." Each time the church gathered to celebrate the Lord's Supper, the people were also remembering their own suffering saints and the larger struggle of Black people for freedom and justice. Holding up the white Communion table covering was an ingenious strategy to teach the next generation to keep alive the memories of all those who were mistreated under the yoke of slavery and Jim Crow.

As has been stated, there is no concrete evidence for documenting the source of this practice. Its wide use in Black Baptist churches may be the result of word-of-mouth or sharing the practice at district, state, and national gatherings. Even so, I assert that this may be a revealed ritual—one given to the Black Church by the living Spirit of the resurrected Jesus. Into the minds and hearts of unknown Black preachers came this gift—

one that enabled them to hear the words of Jesus at one level but hear Jesus also saying to them to encourage their posterity to remember their sufferings by raising the Communion table covering. This was not done to hide the elements on the table from true worshipers but to appeal to their memory, to be keepers of a story that may or may not be written on paper.

When the gathered community of faith sang "What is This?" they were asking a question about the ways in which the Spirit works in the community. When the deacons held up the Communion covering the people knew through instinct and instruction that this was the call to link the past, present, and future. Our ancestors could have sung, "What is this that makes the Communion covering holy? What is this that calls me to remember my mother and my father? What is this that gives me eyes to see the future? Whatever it is, it won't let me hold my peace."

No Black worshiper baptized in the river of struggle and misery can hold their peace about the horrors and hell of slavery. No Black worshiper who had felt the lash of the bullwhip and had known bodily violations can hold back from gathering up the fragments of sacred historical memories, and placing them on the Communion table, symbols of identification of God's own suffering with the people's sufferings.

One possible social experience that connects this practice with the Lord's Supper is the humiliating experience of eating behind a drawn curtain on railway dining cars. It was a practice on trains for the curtain to be drawn to separate a small dining area that seated a handful of Blacks from the main portion of the car that served White passengers. Many Pullman porters who rode the rails to make a living were also deacons in Baptist churches. Is it possible that this practice of raising the Communion covering like a curtain dates back to Pullman porters who were subjected to eating and working behind the infamous segregated curtain?

Could the act of raising the Communion covering like a curtain be perceived as countering the myth of Black inferiority as symbolized in curtains being drawn in railway dining cars? Black worshipers knew that the curtain in law and custom was designed to separate them from Whites and accent their lowly status; however, the raised Communion curtain told a different story. It announced, in essence, that nothing—

not even a drawn curtain on a dining railway car—could separate Black people from God. The drawn curtain—whether in law or custom—was not as powerful as the raised Communion cloth or curtain. The former said "exclusion"; the latter said "inclusion." In a strange twist of irony, whatever sense of self-esteem the segregationist curtain tore down, the Communion covering raised up.

It is significant that the experience of the drawn curtain took place on railway dining cars. At mealtime, Blacks who wanted to eat had to do so behind a curtain that separated Black and white diners. This experience was so pervasive that Blacks who did not ride trains heard the stories about this humiliating experience.

Perhaps the source of this Communion practice has been elusive because the source is in the experience of segregation. Whether it was on trains or other form of public transportation, Black people experienced the curtain. A possible interpretation of the meaning of the act of raising the Communion covering is that Black people took a symbol of separation and integrated it into the saving work of Jesus. What was meant for evil was converted into a symbol that identified Black people's experiences as integral to understanding the power of the gift of the Lord's Supper. What looks like a symbol of continued separation was integrated into the story of God's saving work in the lives of Black people who could identify with the suffering, pain, and death of Jesus.

The raised white sheet on the Communion table sent two messages: 1) It confirmed the reality of suffering in Black people's lives. This was their common bond; 2) The sheet, acting as a curtain, confirmed that their lives mattered and that their experiences of segregation were theological, not simply sociological. Black suffering was a matter of theological depth. God had taken their broken lives and merged them into the salvific story of Jesus. In the spirit of African spiritual ingenuity, Black Baptists took a situation of deep disruption and separation and harnessed it by a process of incorporation and transformation. At the Communion table a symbol of victimization and evil was dismantled, and its powers overcome in the feast of divine salvation.

Wisdom of the Elders

Up to this point this presentation has addressed the progression of my own hypotheses as I searched for answers to the question of the social and theological meanings behind the practice of the deacons holding up the white Communion tablecloth in front of the Communion table.

I turn now to indigenous insights or wisdom from the elders. I sent a letter to several African-American pastors seeking their insights on this Black Baptist Communion practice. In part, the letter stated:

> I have been searching for information on a Communion/Lord's Table practice that I have observed since childhood in some Black Baptist churches. That practice is the act of the deacons holding up the white sheet in front of the communion table while the minister prepares the holy meal. My research has led me to read literature on the disease of consumption in the early part of the twentieth century. I have searched the literature on the history and worship traditions of the Black Church. I have read information on embalming practices in the 1900s and I have sent correspondence to several funeral directors and mortuary science instructors. Empirical evidence is elusive concerning the social origin of this practice. I, therefore, write to ask if you would be gracious enough to provide me with the following:
>
> 1) Reflections on your earliest memories of observing and/or participating in this practice, and
> 2) Reflections on possible social and/or theological meanings of this practice.

Of the responses I received, I share three of them.

Dr. Major L. Jemison, pastor of St. John Baptist Church in Oklahoma City, wrote: "In our tradition, the communion service and the elements have always been held as sacred. Though the cups of grape drink/juice and the wafers are only symbolic, the meaning and the message is treated as if the actual event is being reenacted. It is an attempt to capture the gravity and essence of the experience thereby bringing the congregants into a genuine appreciation for what Christ sacrificed to redeem their souls. Before communion is served a white veil covers the elements. It conveys the purity, the importance and sacredness of the moment. It is understood that the table is not to be touched or moved, nor the trays containing the elements until Communion Service commences. Before communion is served, the minister's hands are washed and towel- dried; white gloves are placed on the hands of each serving deacon; further emphasizing the purity of the moment. The raising of the veil magnifies the reality behind the moment. It takes us beyond the Upper Room to the Crucifixion itself. Its presence as a cover and shield is there to engender thought about the morbid treatment of Christ, the magnitude of His sacrifice as well as, our fraternal commitment to Him. It is our way of preserving the integrity of the moment (personal communication, December 13, 2013).

Reverend Herchel L. Smith, pastor of St. Stephen Community Baptist Church in DeSoto, Texas, wrote: "It's an honor to be asked by you to share what I have been told from my youth up to adulthood about the communion/Lord's Table in the Traditional Black Baptist Church. You won't be able to find this information in books because it's a tradition that's been handed down from generation to generation by Black Baptist preachers. This was a practice that started during slavery.

"The tradition faded with time and was not passed down to the younger preachers of today's society like it was years ago. It is biblical when we think in terms of the bread and the wine. The bread being the representation of the body of Jesus and the wine being the representation of His shed Blood.

"Black people have always been theatrical; we infuse what we see and make it come alive. The older preachers years ago saw the communion table as a casket with a naked body and blood on it. They had the deaconess to prepare the Communion Table so it would look like a body and covered it up with a white sheet.

"When they got ready to administer the communion, the deacons would uncover the body and hold up the white sheet so that no one could see the naked body and the blood. They also believed that the Baptistery represented a Liquid Graveyard, and they were aware of the one who died. This gave the minister a chance to give a Eulogy at the Baptistery and the communion.

"Doctor Spann this was passed on to me as a young preacher by Reverend R. W. McGraw of the Greater Olivet Baptist Church in Los

Angeles, California, and it (is) still in existence today in the old traditional Black Baptist church" (personal communication, November 29, 2013).

Reverend Roosevelt Wright, pastor of New Tabernacle Baptist Church in Monroe, Louisiana, said that "the Communion service is a ritual, a funeral service of Jesus. The cloth separates the eyes of the laity from the majesty of the Lord. The people are not worthy to look upon the body of Jesus until the day he fully reveals himself." Rev. Wright shared that at the True Vine Baptist Church in Monroe, La., the deacons would bring in the Communion table as if it were a coffin. The deacons would march in single file, take two steps, and stop, while lining out the hymn "Guide Me, O, Thou Great Jehovah." The head deacon would lead holding the front of the table. This funeral-like procession may take twenty-five minutes before the Communion table is placed in front of the church (personal communication, June 18, 2014).

Postscript

I began this section by giving some of the questions that birthed my curiosity about the practice of the deacons holding up the white Communion tablecloth while the minister breaks the bread. Two major questions that framed my search were: 1) What might be the origin of this practice, and 2) What are possible social and/or theological meanings of this practice? Several hypotheses were presented as I tracked the progression of my own thoughts and research on the practice. Also, insightful comments were provided by reputable persons, mostly pastors who preside at least monthly at the Lord's Table. These insights confirmed the spiritual depths of this practice either in terms of a respect for mystery or a desire to participate in holiness. Neither of the hypotheses presented nor insights from the elders need to be taken as the closed door on the question of the origin and meaning of this practice. The questions, in spite of these reflections, continue to point in the direction of further reflections and research.

I conclude this chapter with an imaginary sermon as I envision it being delivered in an old-time Black church tradition.

A Sermon: No Flies Landing on the Table
Second Corinthians 5:21

It's good for us to be here this morning;
It's good to see all of you.
You know, somebody didn't wake up this morning,
But God has blessed you and me to see another day.
This ain't no ordinary day; this here is the Lord's Day!
We've come from far and near to partake of the Circament of the Lord's body.
Before I get to my text I just want to say that we are living in an evil world.
There's wars and rumors of wars.
Nations rising up against nations.
The strong against the weak.
The White man against the Black man.
But we are going to make it;
We are going to make it because the Lord is on our side.
Ain't I right about it, children.

The text before us tells us that Jesus, who knew no sin, became sin for us
so that we might become the righteousness of God.
That shows us right there that God had us on his mind all along.
This old world was sinking mighty deep in the mud pit of sin.
But God had pity on us. Hallelujah!
Murder and money were mingled.
Love had taken a holiday.
Kindness couldn't be found.
Truth was hiding around the corner,
But God had mercy on this old hate-filled world.
(*Stay right there! That's mighty good*)

I want to use as the title of this sermon: No Flies Landing on the Table
(That's a good one, pastor)
Recently we have heard talk about a new disease.
This new disease has been called consumption;
Some call it tuberculosis.
It's ravaging the nation;
It's disintegrating families;
It's touched well-kept neighborhoods;
It's in our neck of the woods.
Several antituberculosis leagues have been formed.
I heard the other day that there was talk about one being formed in our vicinity.
You know, I'm for good health.
Our health is all we've got.
God wants us to be healthy.
Even so, some of these nasty diseases are being blamed on us.
Just 'cause we Black, we get to be the burden bearers of bad news.
Well, the way I see it, there are White folks who are sick.
There are Black folks who are sick.
What does it matter who gave it to whom; it's a problem *(Amen)*
It's a problem that's confronting our health.
Now they tell us there are some thangs we can do to cut down on our chances of contracting this horrible illness.
They tell us to clean everything; wipe down everything; get rid of the dirt.
They tell us to keep our windows open and not to sleep with our heads covered.
Now, right there, you know that's a challenge for most of us Black folks *(Alright now)*
They tell us that the carrier of this sickness is flies.
Well, how we gonna get rid of flies? Flies is everywhere.
They swarm the fields; they in the outhouse; they in the church house;
They sit with you when you eat and they fly over you when you sleep.

That's a big size problem to get rid of flies.
But you know, children, this idea come to me. Flies is like sin.
Gossip is like a fly; it poisons things.
Lying is like a fly; it tears up relationships.
Cheating on each other; that's a fly.
Not caring about each other; that's a fly.
Not supporting the program of the church; that's like a fly.
Flies is like sin. (*That's good, Say it)*
You've seen and I've seen dead animals on the road and in the woods.
Unless'n they are removed, what happens?; the vultures gather; flies gather.
That's a picture right there (*Yes it is; that's a good picture)*
When we were dead in sin, the flies clung to us.
Just like some of us is doing now, fanning and swatting at these flies,
We were just swatting at 'em, but it took more than that to deal with them.

Come now to the text.
When flies were buzzing and darting around us and on us, He who knew
no sin became sin for us.
While some us were still in the world, God sent His only begotten Son.
The scent of the world is hard to remove.
Some of us still got the scent of the world on us.
We drink a little bit.
We don't love like we used to.
We don't come to church with a clean heart.
We still got flies to swat (*Yes, sir)*
There are flies swarming in the pews
There are flies in the pulpit.
There are flies on our bodies.
But thanks be to God

There are no flies at the Table,
No flies under the Communion covering.
Flies can't stay here. *(Praise be to God on high)*
While we were waddling in the muck and mire of wrongdoing;
While we were falling short of the glory of God;
While we were zigzagging instead of walking the straight and narrow,
God sent his Son.
That's why we're here this morning.
It's time to get right with God.
God is still calling the roll.
Some day it will be his to call and ours to answer.
We better git right with God, and do it now.
I can't save you; flies are everywhere.
You can't save me; flies are no respecter of person.
Hallelujah! There are no flies landing on the Table.
My job is to shoo away the flies so that we can keep our eyes on Jesus,
the Pioneer and Perfecter of our faith.
I am the shoo-fly man of God sent to announce the Holy Gospel of the resurrection of our Lord.
Look to him, the Author and Finisher of our faith.
He once was dead but is alive forevermore.
He is able to help us and He is able to save.
He can do what no other power can do.
The president of the country has power over the military.
The congress has power to make laws.
The police has power to arrest people.
The courts have power to judge people.
But there is another power; it is the power of God.
God put that power to work on our behalf.
While the world was tumbling further into darkness,
The Son said to the Father: "Send me; I'll go on man's bond."
The Father said to the Son: "If I send you, the world will mistreat you.

They will say all manner of evil against you; they will crucify you."
The Son said to the Father: "Let it be; You have the power to raise me up again."
So, the Father said: "Go, and I will be with you."
Jesus, the Son of God, living in an eternal palatial province of perfect peace,
stepped over the balcony of glory,
started his descent down the rickety ladder of our sin-made condition.
Rung by rung, he came, coming down through forty-two generations.
At the end of each generation, he looked up to his Father and said: "Your will be done."
He came to the world as a baby,
born in Bethlehem,
laid in a manger,
wrapped in swaddling clothes,
visited by shepherds,
worshiped by wise men from the East;
but Mary pondered all these things in her heart.
He grew in stature and in favor with God and man.
At twelve years old he was talking with the elders in the Temple.
At thirty he was baptized in the Jordan.
He tangled with Satan in the wilderness.
He answered the call to do only God's will.
He healed the sick.
He fed the hungry.
He taught the crowds that God is with them.
He confronted the Pharisees and the Sadducees.
He knew that his time had come to go to Jerusalem for the last time.
We know the story. (*Tell the story)*

In the Upper Room with his disciples, he shared bread and cup with them,

and told them to do this each time they gather in remembrance of him.
He said the bread was his body and the cup his shed blood.
The Bible tells us without the shedding of blood there is no remission of sin.
So as we prepare to partake of the Lord's body, let each of us examine ourselves.
We know that there is none righteous but God.
The Scripture says that he became sin so that we might become the righteousness of God.
That's God's hope for us. *(Glory to God)*
There are flies all over the place
But ain't no flies landing on the Table,
No flies under the Communion covering.
No flies where Jesus is.
The flies have been shooed away at the cross,
shooed away all night Friday night; shooed away
all night Saturday, and shooed away come early Sunday morning.
Jesus done been here and gone.
Raised to live forever in his home on high.
Jesus is alive.
He left his Spirit of truth to guide us.
He lives in us.
He is the Wisdom of God.
He is the Source of perfect peace.
He is the Savior of the world.
He is the Bright and Morning Star.
He will pick you up when you fall.
He will make everything alright.
He will guide us until the day is done.
Let's keep our hands in God's hand.
And he will lead us all the way,
Because there are no flies landing on the Table of the Lord.
Hallelujah! Let the church say, Amen.

Chapter Three

CULTURAL PRACTICES AND EXPRESSIONS

Special Days

There are many special days in Black church culture. Like Pine Bluff Baptist Church, many churches marked time by the arrival of these special observances or celebrations. In a real sense, the Black Church Year is made up of these special occasions. The traditional Christian calendar year begins with Advent; however, there are some Black churches that do not utilize the language of the traditional Christian year. Each local church may mark the beginning of the church calendar year at different observances; however, it is common to acknowledge the church's anniversary as the start date. Some churches may mark the beginning and ending of the Black Church calendar with the annual Watch Night service.

The list of observed special days varies, but there seems to be some common ones. A short list would include the following celebrations:

- Pastor's Anniversary or Appreciation
- Church Anniversary
- Choir Anniversary
- Women's Day
- Men's Day
- Friends and Family Day or Homecoming
- Black History Program
- Watch Night

The Pastor's Anniversary or Appreciation

The Pastor's Anniversary or Appreciation is an opportunity for the church and community to recognize the leadership and ministry of the pastor. While this observance is traditional in many Black churches, there are some pastors who may request not to have such a day.

Since the observance is already on the church's calendar, staff and members do not begin planning until the pastor appoints a committee to oversee the program. If done well the previous year, the pastor may appoint the same committee. In some churches, the committee may plan two or three days of worship services, with special guest ministers and choirs, leading up to the Pastor's Anniversary. The pastor invites the guest pastor, who may sometimes be called upon to return for several consecutive years.

The planning committee is also responsible for quietly determining the monetary goal. The financial goal is often divided among organizations or auxiliaries in the church, with each being assigned to raise a designated portion. Some churches are unable to pay the pastor a full-time salary, so the anniversary celebration is a way of catching up or supplementing the pastor's salary.

On the day of the big celebration, if the intended financial goal is not met, there is usually a big push during the Offering period to raise the remaining amount. The Offering period can turn into a big fest in which the presiding guest pastor or appointee is sometimes pressuring the congregation to give more money. The guest pastor may start out by announcing how much his or her congregation is giving. This is done to raise the bar so that others will be encouraged to give liberally. If there are other guest pastors in the pulpit, they give their church's financial gift in a check to the presiding guest pastor who in turn loudly announces the amount of each visiting church's contribution. The presiding guest pastor may challenge the congregation to give "soft" money or "quiet" money, which means dollar bills. Once the goal is reached in the offering, there is a prayer to bless the fruits of the people's generosity. In some cases, the announced amount at the anniversary is not a true reflection of how much the pastor has been given because some members will slip the pastor envelopes with money in them that may not get reported in the total count.

I have known some congregations to give their pastor a vacation or a car as the anniversary gift. Some pastors unashamedly may hint what they want. For example, the pastor may say something like: "My spouse and I have never been on a cruise." This public show of love for the pastor does not go unnoticed in the larger community. Some critics may complain that the pastor is taking money from the church or that the pastor is living high on the hog at the expense of the people. Church members, however, see their gift giving as an expression of love and appreciation for the leadership of the pastor. This seems to be true even if the pastor is not active as a leader in community causes or social justice initiatives. The general perception seems to be that as long as the pastor is taking care of the congregation, then, the flow of love and appreciation continues.

The Church Anniversary

It is important for all churches to take out time to remember how far God has brought them. For churches that were formed shortly after the Civil War or at the end of Reconstruction, this celebration is essential to pass lessons and stories to the next generation. While it is generally true that every church anniversary is an opportunity to celebrate the broad themes of God's grace and providence, those churches that were formed by formerly enslaved persons have stories to tell that are unlike any others. For these persons, the church was indeed the place where they reclaimed their humanity and dignity, and expressed their ingenuity in building a place where they could worship God in their own manner.

The Church Anniversary Committee subdivides its work in terms of subcommittees: souvenir journal, advertisement, program committee, and/or hospitality. For any high day in the life of the church, several announcements are made leading up to the special event. Printed announcements are complemented by verbal announcements from the pulpit, the church's announcement clerk, or from the chairperson of the particular program. The anniversary day is "talked up" by the pastor and members in order to solicit the broadest support in terms of attendance and finance.

A distinctive piece of the anniversary celebration is the reading of the church's history. Most often the formal history of the church, regardless of its size or location, is usually limited to one or two pages in the Church Anniversary program. Unfortunately, too many Black churches have not written their history in a book length format. The limited history that is written in the anniversary booklet or program is usually the same every year, with the exception of changing or adding a name, as appropriate. There are some Black churches that have designated church historians or a Church History Committee. The Church History Committee is responsible for regularly meeting throughout the year to update the history and to make it available to church members.

In my judgment, it is better for a local church to have an active church history committee than to assign the task to one person. The church history committee would have a designated place in the church where the records are securely archived. It is not a good idea for one person to be the keeper of the church's history. I have seen single member historians behave as if the records belong to them, and will challenge anyone who wants to engage in serious research to substantiate the history or enlarge upon it. I have known church records to be destroyed when one or two people negatively exercise their power.

Choir Anniversary

The Choir Anniversary is another way to celebrate and recognize the work of singers and musicians who lead the church in praise of God. This idea emerged during the time when most rural churches had only one choir. Even as other choirs were created, the Choir Anniversary celebration is one day of praise and gratitude for all the choirs that compose the music ministry.

Choir anniversaries are first and foremost worship opportunities. Secondly, they are platforms to recognize the gifts of musicians and choir members. Thirdly, they are fundraisers to assist in meeting the budget of a church. With any anniversary where there is a financial goal, people will work hard to raise the money through raffle tickets, selling dinners, and giving extra at the Offering time. Whenever a self-imposed financial goal is reached, the people are empowered to know that they can work together to reach goals, whether financial or otherwise. Moreover, it is considered a testament to the leadership of the Anniversary committee, through the various subcommittees, when the special day is a success. The church also views the reaching of financial goals as an indication of having a good pastoral leader.

Women's Day

The pioneer of Women's Day among Black Baptists was Nannie Helen Burroughs. She advocated for this day in Baptist churches because women needed a platform to express their oratorical gifts and share their ideas on topics of interest to the whole church and to women. While raising money became a major agenda item, Burroughs wanted women to raise up their heads and voices, and not be confined to the offices traditionally assigned to them by male church leaders.

On Women's Day, the worship experience is led by women; however, I have seen some Women's Day programs in which male pastors were involved. In Baptist churches that have not progressed to acknowledge God's call to women, the speaker may not be allowed to deliver the speech from the pulpit but from the main floor of the sanctuary. This was, and in some instances, still is, a power play backed up by a theology of excluding women from the sacred office of proclaiming God's word. Although sexist in nature, there are occasions when a woman gives the address followed later in the same service by a man who delivers the sermon. If the speaker for Women's Day is a layperson, she is usually someone who is believed to be a role model in her field, and someone young girls can look to as an example of leadership.

The unity of women on this day is often signaled by the coordination of colors for the day. Women may be asked to wear certain colors, as chosen by the Women's Day committee. Many women await the announcement of the color scheme so that they can know if they need to purchase a new outfit for the occasion. Wearing African attire on this day is in vogue in many churches. This particular attire is an opportunity for many women to support women-owned stores that sell African clothing.

While Burroughs' initial aim was to elevate women through public speaking, many churches still pour tremendous energies into fundraising.

Women network in small groups to sponsor activities such as, teas, brunches, style shows, musicals, and dinners. In some churches, a bazaar may be set up for Black women entrepreneurs to sell their items, such as, books, jewelry, hair products, clothes, CDs, etc. If the guest speaker has written a book or has a CD for sell, this is an occasion to promote them. The goal of a financial drive on this day may be to contribute to the general revenue of the church, or in some churches, assist in funding college scholarships.

In some churches, men support Women's Day by serving as ushers, helping with transportation, and cooking the meal following the celebration.

Men's Day

In churches that do not ordain women, it could be said that every Sunday is Men's Day since men are almost always in charge of leading the worship service.

Men's Day is an opportunity for men to use their gifts in service to God in worship and to lift up role models for young men. Some of the men who may lead in a worship celebration may be standing in the pulpit or before the congregation for the first time in a public speaking role.

This day also provides a platform for the leadership of the Men's ministry to call forth inactive men to get involved in the group's activities. Men's general ministry activities may include some of the following: singing in a choir, ushering, participating in a Bible study, serving on the parking lot team, mentoring young men, assisting with providing meals to persons in need, and visiting nursing homes and jails. Activities for men leading up to Men's Day may include: a musical or concert, a church-wide dinner, a retreat, or prayer services led by men.

Family and Friends Day

This day may also be called Family Day, Big Day, or simply, Homecoming. It is an opportunity to invite as many family members and friends as possible to celebrate kinship in God's family. When this special day is held in the afternoon, there is a guest pastor who brings a choir, but there may also be special music from other choirs or soloists. There is generally a festive mood that uplifts the entire service. A feature of this day is the meal. This is a time for men and women of the church to cook their favorite dishes. There is often too much food, so many guests carry take-out plates with them.

Black History Observance

Dr. Carter G. Woodson, the originator of Black History Week (now Black History Month), envisioned a time in which African Americans' contributions to the world would be celebrated. While it is true that Black History is observed in the shortest month of the year, it is not true that February was selected because of its length. Rather, February was the month in which Abraham Lincoln and Frederick Douglas were born. Speakers with an African consciousness never tire of reminding audiences that Black history did not begin in 1619, but that Black history begins on the continent of Africa, where human civilization began. Just as Black history cannot be limited to a calendar date, neither can it be confined to a month. In truth, Black history is an ongoing reality.

Churches celebrate Black History Month in several ways. These include:

- Skits or plays that reenact pivotal events, e.g., the Montgomery Bus boycott
- Orations by young people. Popular poems include "The Creation" by James Weldon Johnson and "Still I Rise" by Maya Angelou
- Incorporating the Spirituals in the choir's repertoire
- Designing litanies or responsive readings that highlight Black experiences and values
- Hanging portraits of important figures throughout the church
- Sponsoring a lecture series with a noted author/scholar
- Preaching that emphasizes African American history.

The importance of telling our true history is poignantly expressed in an account I received from a student. A survivor of the Holocaust had her number stamped on her arm. When asked what it represented, she shared that it was the symbol of her time spent in a concentration camp in Germany. The number etched into her skin was a visible reminder of the reality of human suffering and her near-death experience. After telling her own truth about that horrible experience, someone doubted her truth by saying that it was cleverly created to solicit sympathy and to trash Germany. This woman told a more startling experience: her own family members did not believe her experience was as awful as they had been told. Wow!

We must continue to teach our children about the struggles that African Americans have endured in every segment of this society. May we never hear our children or grandchildren say to us that living through the era of Jim Crow could not have been that bad. Better still, may we never hear them say that they thought slavery never really happened!

Watch Night Service

At my home church, Pine Bluff Baptist Church, the members gathered to watch the old year out and the New Year in. The church always had a meal before the service—a meal in which there had to be black-eyed peas, greens, cornbread, and few other traditional dishes. It was believed that black-eyed peas brought good luck for the coming year. Many African Americans still eat chitlins (chitterlings) and cornbread on New Year's Day. What was once confined to a few families that ate them, chitterlings can now be bought in grocery stores or meat packing stores. When our foreparents were in the bonds of slavery, they killed hogs for the plantation owners who got the best of the meat, and left the intestines and the head, unwanted parts, to enslaved persons. We learned to eat chitlins as part of our survival in slavery. Eating it once a year is a reminder of our ancestors' strength to overcome. The members of Pine Bluff Baptist Church would congregate around nine o'clock at night for food and fellowship, and then spend the rest of the time up until midnight singing, praying, testifying, and hearing the word of God proclaimed. At midnight, the congregation would be on their knees or in an attitude of prayer thanking God for blessing them to see another year. After entering the New Year in prayer, the members wished each other well in the New Year with generous hugs and handshakes.

During my childhood, the meaning of this celebration was not lost on the members of Pine Bluff. For members of my home church, being descendants of formerly enslaved persons meant that Watch Night service had a historical connection to Lincoln's Emancipation Proclamation. Black people gathered to watch the old year out and the New Year in, but they also met on the eve of freedom to embrace the good news that slavery's chains had broke at last! Of all the blessings that Black people thanked God for, their chief gratitude was the blessing of human freedom.

Dressing up on Sunday

As has been stated, as I was growing up, we had Sunday clothes and shoes—a way of signifying the sacredness of the day as well as our self-respect and acceptance. This was particularly true when most churchgoers worked manual labor jobs that did not require formal or professional dress. All weeklong, Brother John or Sister Jane may have worked hard from sunup to sundown in the fields, at a factory, or on an assembly line in hot conditions, and were not addressed as Mr. or Mrs. But when Sunday came, they transformed themselves into office holders in the only institution to which they could claim was theirs. In the church they had titles such as, Superintendent of the Sunday School, chairman of the Deacon Board, or president of the Missionary Society. In their own institution they addressed one another as Brother or Sister or Deacon or Elder. Through titles, offices, and clothing, Black people took back their dignity and self-esteem. Black men took special care to wear clean, pressed suits; and women, likewise, took special care to look nice. Many women accented their spiritual sense of self by wearing hats. There was a time when church hats carried with it a status that demanded respect. In an earlier day the pastor's wife was expected to wear fashionable hats as a way of setting the tone for the dignity of all women. In this sense, many church women would not be seen in church without a hat. Both men and women may have expressed themselves through matching outfits and accessories. Matching items made a statement that shouted not only the person's self-respect but the respect the person accorded to the gathered community of faith.

It is common to see the importance of dress in the uniforms, dress, or robes worn by ushers or choir members. When ushers don the same colors or clothing, they are signaling their special role in helping to order the worship experience. Again, dressing up in matching uniforms or attire is not to be taken lightly. This is more than a power statement in fashion; it is a call to expect something significant to happen in this worship space that is different from what takes place in other venues. Occasionally when ushers or choir members' well-placed attire catches the pastor's attention, he or she may offer words of praise to the group. Being noticed or publicly praised in this way means something to those who may have gone out of their way to participate in the effort to coordinate dress or attire.

It has been a contemporary trend for churches to promote Sundays when people are encouraged to dress casually. This is a way of symbolizing that the church is open to all people. There is an unenforceable standard for dress even when people are invited to come casually. No one is going to ask someone to leave for wearing a particular clothing item, but there will be some eyes cutting them down as well as quiet conversations in the pews. I recall a passionate criticism that was shared with me by a mother of the church who could not believe that some young women would come to church without stockings. When it comes to casual dress in the church, either we mean what we say or we say only what we mean.

Honoring Elders

It is important that elders be treated with respect and dignity in the church and in society. Many of them have experienced just about every conceivable loss or encounter with injustice and discrimination. They have been where we are going. It is equally important to hear their stories and to share them especially in youth ministry settings. Unlike the era in which I grew up, young people may call older persons by their first name. Each older member has to decide her or his level of comfort or acceptance of being addressed by a youth on a first-name basis. Some pastors, following the trend in Hip-Hop culture, began to self-identify using an initial in their name, e.g. Pastor T or Pastor B. This is acceptable as long as a child of the church when asked in another setting the name of the pastor is able to give the complete first and last name of the pastor.

Historically, most Black pastors in the early part of the twentieth century wrote their first and middle initials along with the surname.

Initials are used consistently in written records because Black men were not addressed as Mr. and Black women were not addressed as Mrs. The strategy of everyone giving their names as initials was intended to get respect by having to be called Mr. Jones or Mrs. Smith.

In a youth-oriented culture, it is also important to have a balanced emphasis in ministry so that elders don't feel excluded. Many retired elders can still participate in active ministries. There are always wise ones in the congregation who can give the pastor a heads-up on things.

It is also true that many older church members may serve in church positions for their entire lives. There may be complaints that some elders are in the way or that they may need to step aside, but a wise pastor knows that she or he has to work with them and sometimes around them to carry on the ministry of the church. I attended a Women's Day program at a local church in which the congregation was honoring an eighty-year old member for her service in the Missionary Society. At eighty, she was stepping down after having served as president for decades.

Just as there is a youth ministry in the church, there is the need for an organized senior adult or ministry for/with the elders. This ministry may include field trips, educational opportunities, outreach to a school, as well as recording the stories of elders on video and in writing. The church contends that wisdom resides in the elders, and that wisdom needs to be passed on. An intentional approach to gathering and distributing this wisdom is itself an act of wisdom. After an elder transitions "from labor to reward," that wisdom is gone if there has not been an intentional effort to interview and record that person's story.

Church Mothers

In Baptist circles this title is not an official status, although it is bestowed with some privileges. A Church Mother is not an elected position; it is an honorary title given to older women who have faithfully served the church. There is no age in which the title is given. Whenever this title is given, it gives the bearer a responsibility to offer guidance to the young. The privilege of the title is that a Church Mother may be looked to in a church meeting for a sense of approval. A nod from her means more than words can convey. Church Mothers are addressed as Mother instead of Sister. Through longevity, experience, and respect in the church, she has transitioned from being called Sister to being addressed as Mother. I have been on the parking lot of a church that had several parking spaces reserved for "Church Mothers."

Titles

As hard as some pastors try to deemphasize titles in the church, the fact is that titles are important in the Black Church. A pastor's effort to neutralize titles is driven by the spirit of equality. A pastor may want everyone to feel like they are on a level playing field, but the reality is that titles are not going away.

Among Black Baptist pastors, the title "Doctor" is pronounced as an honorary gesture. A person who is not a seminary graduate or may only have a high school diploma may be called "Doctor" by friends out of deference for preaching prowess. The respect given to a person in this category is equal to the respect and admiration given to someone who has an earned doctorate from an accredited institution.

In addition to the community-bestowed moniker of "Doctor," there is also the use of the title "Bishop" in Baptist and nondenominational settings. In denominations with an Episcopal system, a pastor may be elected a bishop and assigned an Episcopal area of supervision. One justification for the use of the title Bishop in Baptist and nondenominational settings is that the word can be translated as teacher, one who is responsible for equipping the saints for the work of ministry. While this appropriation of the meaning of the term may be correct, many pastors have gone beyond the teaching limit to impose an authority for hierarchical governance.

Honoring the First Family

It is a tradition in Black churches that have male pastors for the spouse to be referred to as the First Lady. She is accorded special honor and respect. She may have a parking space reserved for her. Ushers are attentive to her and may escort her to her seat which is usually near the front. Whenever she walks in she is given special attention as members observe her dress. She is expected to set the tone by working cooperatively with all the members of the church. On special occasions, especially Women's Day, she is expected to support the cause by wearing the colors for the day, and she may be called upon to introduce the guest preacher. There have been pastors who have not endeared themselves to the congregation but because the church loved the pastor's wife, the church followed the leadership of the pastor.

There are Baptist women pastors who may or may not be married. In either case, the church extends the same love and respect to the pastor's family. A male spouse is expected to be involved in men's ministries and to set a supportive tone for the church. The church wants to get to know the pastor's children by name and to be supportive of them in their personal endeavors. While it is hard for some pastor's children to be in a glass house, most church folks understand that being a pastor's kid does not mean that they have to forego being children or teenagers. There can be drama in the pastor's house just as there can be drama in any church member's house.

Ritual for Receiving Tithes and Offerings

When my wife visited South Africa, she attended several worship services in African Methodist Episcopal churches. She brought back pictures, but the ones I remember most are of African worshipers dancing in the pews and in the aisles as they brought their offerings to support the church. They slapped their money on the table much like a domino player slaps a domino on the table. They were bringing their offerings with great joy.

In many Black churches, before the offering is received the pastor makes an appeal to give. The appeal is often for people to give more, over and beyond what they have decided to give. Sometimes the appeal is grounded in generous words of gratitude for the people's generosity. More often the appeal is prefaced with verses from the Bible. An almost universal one is: "The Lord loves a cheerful giver." Sometimes the pastor will put it in the form of question and response: "The Lord loves what kind of giver?" And the people respond, "a cheerful giver." It is fairly common for the announcement of the Offering to be received with clapping and verbal expressions of joy.

In the church of my childhood, during the offering time, the ushers would come forward to give directions to the various sections of the congregation. All tithers were asked to come first. There was an offering receptacle shaped like a church building where tithers placed their money. After the tithers, the pastor called for regular offerings. In each case the people marched around the sanctuary to the Offering table and back to their pews. The pastor would sometimes instruct people who did not have anything to give to come and lay their hands on the table. There was no embarrassment in having to do so. This instruction was given with no theological justification. On the surface it sounds like a meaningless gesture. Could the invitation to come and place your hand on the table be a symbolic sign of faith that when God does bless with resources to give the person will be in the habit of giving?

In churches that distribute the Offering tray in the pews, an established protocol is for ushers not to make change during the offering; members are not to make their own change as the offering tray is being passed around. Visitors who may not know the protocol are given their change by the attending usher at the end of the Offering period.

Church Ushers

It is a Black church colloquialism to pronounce the word usher as "urrsher." Sometimes spoken in playful jest, all members recognize the importance of the ministry of ushering. One of the first persons that worshipers meet at the door is an usher.

I have heard stories of ushers being verbally abused at the entrance into the sanctuary as members want to get in at the time when it is not appropriate. Sometimes ushers may direct members to another section of the sanctuary, but some members will brush by to find a seat in a section that is already filled. A regular issue that ushers deal with is late-comers who want the person sitting on the end of the pew to move down while the person on the end of the pew came early so that she or he could sit in that place.

Ushers may be divided by boards. For example, a church may have Usher Board #1, Usher Board #2, Youth Ushers, etc. Every church Usher Corps has a head usher—one who directs the others. Ushers meet on a regular basis to practice their choreography so that worship attendees have a pleasant worship experience. Ushers move through the aisles with dignity and grace without calling unnecessary attention to themselves. They are part of the ambience of worship. On Communion Sunday they are an impressive group to watch, especially in a large sanctuary with ushers and communion assistants combined. On First Sunday it is traditional for women ushers to wear white and for men to dress in a dark suit, white shirt, and matching tie.

Ushers have their own signals for communicating. There are signals for closing and opening doors; for moving when the pastor stands to read the Scripture and announce the sermon title; for indicating when a section of the sanctuary is filled; for indicating how many more persons can be seated on a pew; and for indicating an emergency or need for medical assistance.

In some congregations there are pulpit ushers, persons assigned to respond to requests or needs from the pastor and other pulpit ministers. Sometimes notes may be passed to the pastor to make a late announcement; to announce that someone has left their car lights on; or to announce special guests in attendance.

Sample Letter of Invitation to a Guest Preacher

The purpose of this sample letter is to highlight the invitation for the guest preacher to address the theme and the biblical text as decided upon by the anniversary committee.

> Dear Pastor Smith,
>
> It was good to briefly visit with you at this year's State Congress of Christian Education in Beaumont. Liberty Baptist Church members who went as delegates had nothing but high praise for your closing sermon. As a matter of fact, your message, along with your commitment to social justice, led us to enter into a conversation with our pastor, Rev. Jones, about inviting you to be

this year's preacher for Liberty's Church Anniversary Service. The Service is scheduled for October 30 at 3:30pm.

After consultation with Pastor Jones and the Church Anniversary Committee, I am pleased to invite you to be this year's preacher. I trust that your schedule allows you to offer an affirmative reply. After much deliberation and prayer, the committee was led to the following theme and Scripture for the occasion: Theme__________; Scripture ________.

Pastor Jones and the Committee trust that this invitation is arriving in plenty of time for you to be in deep prayer and meditation as you prepare a fresh word for this special occasion. We will be lifting up the theme and the Scripture in prayer as we anticipate your response.

Also, you will receive an honorarium in the amount of $_________.

A reply no later than August 15 is greatly appreciated. Please send your email reply to me and copy Pastor Jones. We require a written reply so that the Church History Committee may have it to place in the records.

We hope to see you, the members of your congregation, along with one of your choirs and an Usher Board, on October 30.

The Hospitality Ministry will have dinner prepared for you and other guests in the fellowship hall at 2:15pm.

Sincerely,

Chairperson of the Church Anniversary Committee

This sample letter contains everything an invited guest preacher needs to know. Another correspondence should be sent as a friendly reminder. Busy pastors who are being invited may need more than one form of communication to remind them. I have had the unfortunate experience of an organization sending me an invitation to speak using only one form of media, and I saw it too late to offer an affirmative reply.

Hymns/Songs of Zion

One of the gifts that Pine Bluff Baptist Church gave me was a rich treasury of hymns and other songs of Zion. We sang lined hymns led by a deacon or one of the mothers of the church. A lined hymn is where the leader gives a few words of the song, and the congregation slowly sings and moans those same words, the pitch being set by the leader at the end of each phrase. My generation of churchgoers learned a collection of so-called "Standby" hymns. They were called standby because these were songs that were passed on from one generation to the next. These songs were sure to open the windows of the soul and let God's fresh, reviving wind blow through the congregation. A short list of these amazing songs includes:

- Blessed Assurance
- Amazing Grace
- Precious Lord
- What a Fellowship
- At the Cross
- Father, I Stretch My Hands to Thee
- I Want Jesus to Walk with Me
- Is Your All on the Altar?
- Jesus, Keep Me Near the Cross
- Oh, How I Love Jesus
- Pass Me Not, O Gentle Savior
- Shine on Me
- Yield Not to Temptation.

Due to the heavy emphasis on contemporary gospel songs, many young churchgoers do not know the hymns and songs that brought us over after slavery and through the Jim Crow era. Young people need us to inform them by regularly singing them in worship. A former Minister of Music shared with me that a friend of hers, also a Minister of Music at a large Black church, asked for the words to "O Come All Ye Faithful." The inquiring Minister of Music had heard the words but did not know the full text; neither did the inquiring Minister of Music know that the words could be found in the hymnal in the back of the pew. I was visiting a church when Bishop Leontine Kelly was the guest preacher. She began by quoting the words of a beautiful hymn. The congregation wildly responded with Amens as if those were the words of a contemporary poet. The person sitting next to me did not realize that she was quoting from a hymn that was in the church's hymnal.

Today's popular gospel songs put a lot of stress on individual praise and personal blessings from God, almost to the exclusion of social justice concerns. The theological themes of justice, freedom, struggle, and equality need to be put back in the vocabulary of contemporary gospel/praise music. Contemporary musical composers and theologically informed pastors are challenged to put social justice sermons into songs, liberation theology into tunes and texts of truth, and verses that give vitality to a vision of God's reign on earth.

The following two songs reflect the merger of the social and the spiritual. The first is titled "We Are the Ones."

We are the ones who must answer the call
When the fulfillment of civil rights is forestalled
Do what we must to defend our sacred worth,
In freedom's prosperous bank there's no dearth.

We are the ones who must teach the young
And show them where they come from
This is not a time for show, form, and fashion.
Children need to see and hear our family's devotion.

We are the ones who model purpose
With strength and assurance to disclose
The rich resources of our living history
For the young this should not be a mystery.

We are the ones to span the divide
And never lose focus but keep our stride.
The way ahead may not always be straight
With God we will make it through the narrow gate.

The second song is titled "Every Child is Precious."

Every child is precious in God's sight
In every soul there is a light
No one is born before God's time
The Creator's work is all sublime
We are different in many ways
Diversity enriches all our days
Color and class may seek to divide
The image of God is nothing to hide
Male and female in equal standing
Together in unity at Eden's landing
The tree of life grows in every garden
Where dreams of justice have not hardened
No one race by God's design is superior
No one race by human design is inferior
Every branch on God's living tree
Is born in love to be free
The only good chain is arm in arm
Where we trust and there's no harm.

Pulpit Attendants

It is not unusual for some pastors to have volunteer laypersons who attend to the pastor and spouse's needs while they are at church. A popular term for these persons is armor-bearer. I have seen laymen serve in the role of "bodyguards" or ushers for the pastor. When the pastor drives up to his or her assigned parking space, these individuals will come to the car to greet the pastor and family. They may offer to carry the pastor's briefcase into the office. They may station themselves outside the office in order to respond to any wish or request from the pastor. I have seen laypersons assume the task of ensuring that the pastor's Bible and sermon notes are placed in the pulpit before the beginning of the worship experience. The armor-bearers or attendants are especially attentive whenever the pastor exits the pulpit; they exit with the pastor to offer a modicum of protection from interruptions. At a revival that I attended, the guest revivalist referred to her attendant as her cloak-bearer. The cloak-bearer's role is to be sure that the revivalist has everything she needs. Sitting on the front row, the attendant or cloak-bearer is a sure-fire source of an Amen. After the preacher has finished preaching, the cloak-bearer enters the pulpit to assist the preacher in putting on a coat, a cloak, or shawl. The cloak is to keep the perspiring preacher from catching a cold from a cool draft in the sanctuary.

During one of James Brown's legendary onstage performances, he would be wringing wet with perspiration, and one of his attendants would come on stage and throw a large coat over his shoulders as he continued his enthusiastic, "can't help it," routine. Crowds often wildly responded to this showmanship because, many of them being church-goers, first witnessed this in a Spirit-filled, shouting, worship experience.

Three Oral Expressions

There are many church-related expressions that are used by pastors. I turn now to three of them. The first is the place called *Flunkersville.* This is the place where every preacher has visited. This is where the sermon flunks, or at least, this is the perception from the preacher's point of view. A seasoned pastor, acting in the role of mentor, may not say to a preacher that he flunked but will encourage the preacher to pray harder and study some more. No preacher is perfect all the time; however, preaching excellence is the standard every Sunday. After fifty years of preaching, I realize that Flunkersville did not stop me from giving God my best the next time. It can be a place of self-flagellation, a place where the preacher wants to question the call, but, inevitably, the Spirit revives the truly called preacher's soul. It is an awful feeling to be preaching and know that you are sinking or flunking. I have seen some singing preachers try to get out of Flunkersville by singing and whooping one of those sure-fire songs that gets people shouting. I have learned that Flunkersville is a place of growth and learning; it does not have to travel with us, but its lessons should follow us into new classroom experiences where the standard of excellence is refined.

I grew up in a preaching tradition that tested a young preacher's calling by announcing in the worship service that the young preacher is going to deliver the word. I have been tested and refined in this tradition many times. It can be a heart-racing experience to be in the pulpit expecting to hear the pastor preach and the pastor announces that you are the preacher. Experience in this tradition has taught me to always be ready to preach. I share two experiences of being called on to preach at the very last minute in a worship service.

When I was a student at Bishop College, I caught the bus to Marshall to attend a revival because I wanted to hear the guest revivalist. When I arrived at the Galilee Baptist Church, I was warmly greeted by Pastor O. C. Rollins. When it was time to leave the office and go into the service, he and I had prayer, even though the guest preacher was presumably on his way from Shreveport, Louisiana. As the worship service progressed, Rev. Rollins left the pulpit to see if the revivalist was driving up in the parking lot. He returned to announce that it does not seem that the guest preacher will be here. He then said to his congregation, "But there is a young man here from Bishop. He is no stranger here. I am going to ask him to preach." Rev. Rollins then invited me back to his office where I was able to gather my thoughts. I had notes for a sermon in my Bible. When he and I returned to the pulpit, the choir led in singing "Amazing Grace," and afterwards I was up declaring God's word.

Shortly after my wife and I married, we moved to North Little Rock where I took a teaching assignment at a college and later accepted a pastoral assignment. We were frequent visitors at a church near the college. One night the church was holding a special service that was very well-attended by lay and clergy. The service was lively in all its acts of praise. When the time came for the preaching of the gospel, the pastor went to the pulpit and spoke these words: "The Spirit is telling me that Brother Spann has a word for us. After the choir sings one more selection, the next voice you hear will be that of Reverend Spann. Let the church say Amen." Without skipping a beat, I reached for my Bible, turned to a passage, and within a few minutes I was up preaching. I could stand up preaching because Flunkersville had long been in my rearview mirror.

The second expression is: "*govern yourselves accordingly.*" Many Baptist pastors spoke this expression following the announcement which was read by the Church Clerk. The meaning is clear: participate, attend, support, or give. The pastor cannot make people attend, support, or give, or behave in a certain way. The essence of the appeal is to the discipline of self-government. The governor of human behavior and decisions is the self-- the self that is now a member of Christ's body. As the invitation to govern the self is extended, the pastor is really appealing to each church member to remember that the self is governed ultimately by the Spirit of Christ who is the Head of the Church. This appeal is not intended to put people on a guilt trip because there are some real practical factors that inhibit some people from attending or participating or giving. My interpretation of this appeal is: look carefully at your life circumstances to see if you can govern yourselves accordingly. A careful look may lead a person to conclude that she or he can attend or participate or support or give. If not, there is always the next time.

The third expression is: "*We have done as the Lord has commanded and yet there is room.*" My father in the ministry, Rev. Joseph Cooper, would make this statement in his closing remarks. He never explained its meaning. The one instance where I have found this expression is in the context of supporting the work of building educational facilities for college students in the late nineteenth century. Most Black colleges got their start in this period. College officials wanted to be able to say to all students that there was plenty good room for them. In the context in which Pastor Cooper spoke this expression, the underlying sense was that while we have had a good time in the Lord, there is always more that each of us can do in the kingdom of God.

Leadership Images: Lay and Clergy

Avoider of conflict. This is someone whose personality does not easily engage criticism or sharp differences between people. Where a leader might be expected to step in and offer direction, this leader has a hands-off or look-the-other way posture. Conflict avoidance does not necessarily mean the problem will go away. It means delay, and sometimes in the delay new and thornier issues may arise.

Authoritarian. This image of leadership is associated with being fully in control, wanting to be the judge and arbiter of all decisions. There is little or no room for negotiation or new points of view. The final verdict is with the leader. A strong leader may be associated with this image, but there are other examples of strength in leadership that are open to other peoples' ideas.

Insecure. Insecurity is more of an attitude than an image, but if a leader is consistently viewed as jealous of other people's gifts, then the people's perception of the leader translates into a leadership image. An insecure or jealous leader sees gifts in others as a threat instead of a resource that can strengthen her or his leadership.

People-pleaser. This is an image of leadership that is similar to avoider of conflict. A people-pleaser may find it hard to say no in order to be liked. Being liked is an internal driver of decision-making. The fault in this image is that a leader is not going to be liked by all the people all the time. A smiling face of a supporter today may turn into a frowning critic tomorrow.

Go-to public figure. There are lay and clergy community leaders who are sought out for their comments in times of controversy in a city. If the leader happens to be in charge of a large organization, that leader is especially called upon to address critical issues. There are dozens of community leaders in a city but somehow one or two get chosen as the go-to persons. The people in political power in a city or in the media, for example, may decide that one or two leaders in a community may be the ones worthy of their concentrated attention. Leaders selected by local politicians, business leaders, and/or the media may not be persons that are chosen by the community as their spokespersons.

Gospel preacher. There are pastors who primarily see themselves as gospel preachers. Pastoring a church is the means by which they get to exercise the call to preach. Over time, a tenured pastor may be revered more as a traveling evangelist than as a pastor. Pastors who conduct several revivals a year may be an example of this image.

Solo leader. This is a person who acts on her or his own ideas or visions without necessarily consulting with others. There is in this type of leadership a weakness in seeing their weakness. People around the leader may see things falling apart while the leader charges full speed ahead with no sense of the consequences. Sometimes the smartest person in the room is not in the room, but a narcissistic leader cannot see it.

Traditionalist. A traditionalist follows the pattern that has been set. This leader's attitude is: There is no need to change something if it has worked this long. The mantra of this leader is: "If ain't broke, don't fix it!"

Hype master. This is a leader with energy and intelligence to get a crowd excited about accomplishing a goal or a vision. Repetitive use of language and personal enthusiasm are means of maintaining the public's belief in a vision. This image can turn negative when the leader does not have the organizational ability or theological resources to realize and sustain a verbalized vision.

Innovator. Unlike the traditionalist, this is an image of a leader who is creative and productive. The innovator is not afraid to try something new. This leader does not have to be the genesis of every new idea but is willing to listen and encourage others to get out of their comfort zone.

Behind-the-scene. There are people in every organization, especially churches, who see themselves as calling the shots behind the scene. They are knowledgeable of what is going on and try to control outcomes through people with whom they are connected. These may be people who were once in power but are no longer in power but who attempt to manipulate outcomes through unhealthy interference.

Partial investor. This is a leader who is not fully invested in the leadership of the organization. There are full-time pastoral leaders who do not want to work hard. They may carve out their level of leadership involvement to the exclusion of ministry areas that would normally be expected of them. Partial investors are more focused on the next opportunity to get ahead than on their present assignment.

Mentor. This is a leader who wants to pass on to others lessons learned from her or his experience. A mentor looks for opportunities to share leadership and knowledge. Good pastoral mentors can boast of having many "daughters or sons in the ministry." A secure mentor is not intimidated by the gifts of others but is willing to provide opportunities for those gifts to be expressed.

Teacher. There was a time in the Black Church when it was said that those who were not good at preaching went into teaching. This was an in-house assessment that did not value preachers whose style was that of a teacher. Because the preacher did not come with a lot of emotional flare, the judgment among the person's peers was that she or he is a good teacher. Today there is a need for and an acceptance of gifted teaching preachers. Worshipers want to have their hearts warmed and their minds stretched.

Social justice advocate. This is a leader who understands the biblical mandate regarding doing justice. Also, the leader knows the import of history, and is committed to challenging and transforming institutions built on a legacy of systemic injustice. The leader who advocates social justice does not limit her or his vision to societal institutions, exclusive of the church, but includes practices and theologies in religious institutions that block the fulfillment of equality, dignity, and human worth.

Funerals

Death is viewed as a part of life. Some common phrases that I have heard Black people speak include: "the deceased paid a debt that we all must pay," and that "God is calling the roll." Whether viewed as paying a debt or answering the roll, death is inevitable and is faced in many ways.

In evangelical hymns and sermons, church members were reminded to prepare for the afterlife. Choirs sang about streets paved with gold or about walking around heaven all day or about seeing loved ones gone on before or about a heavenly mansion. These so-called "otherworldly" songs reminded Christian pilgrims that this world is not their home. Visions of a new life without pain, sickness, or trouble, were proclaimed by Black preachers with such passion and power that the people responded with leaps, cries, and shouts of joy. Each person sitting under the sound of the preacher's voice knew that they had to get their house in order, for "soon and very soon we are going to see the King."

This type of evangelical view of death and the afterlife has not been without its contemporary theological critics. The hope in the afterlife has a tendency to depoliticize investment in doing all one can to transform social structures on behalf of justice. Investment in social justice is viewed to be more significant than waiting to put on some golden slippers over in glory. Life here on earth is the beginning of eternal life. The theology of the "sweet by and by" does not encourage church members to raise their hands to remove the yoke of burden. Instead, they often succumb to dreaming of a day when the burdens of this life will be over. A theological truth, however, is that life is dynamic, processive; it continues beyond the grave. God is the author of life, and God is alive now and forevermore.

Black women freedom fighters like Sojourner Truth, Fannie Lou Hamer, and Ida B. Wells-Barnett could stand up for justice because they knew that God wanted them to make a difference in this life. They had conquered the fear of death because of their encounter with the living God who gave them the strength to act in defiance of racial injustices. They believed human deeds have eternal consequences.

Death in the Black Church encompasses many differing features. I present what I consider to be common features of Black funerals.

Attention Given to How the Deceased Looks

A common remark at the "Wake" or during general visitation hours is how the deceased looks. Viewers may say, "She sure looks natural," or "He looks peaceful." Care is given to how the deceased looks in terms of facial features and the manner of dress. The matter of facial features takes into consideration that the person did not die a violent death, for example in a mangled car wreck. Even if a Black body suffered a violent end, Black morticians understand the cultural necessity of viewing the body. Some Black family members may be concerned that a light-skinned or fair-skinned deceased relative not look too dark. Another cultural concern is hair—in life and in death. Black morticians and hairdressers know how to work with Black hair—whether natural or a wig. Moreover, care is given to dressing the deceased. Family members may buy a new dress or suit for the deceased even when the deceased has a suit or a dress that may be appropriate. Selecting a beautiful casket is significant because the community is looking to see how the deceased is being "put away." If things are done well in terms of facial features, hair, dress, and casket selection, a regular assessment is that the deceased was "put away nicely". This is an affirmation that the family did not cut corners or try to have a cheap funeral. The community standard was upheld.

Attendance

Attendance may be a measure of the length and breadth of influence the deceased had. Black mourners pay attention not only to how many people attended but who attended. Family members want to know if their loved one's life mattered beyond kith and kin, and this is often measured by the attendance of friends, neighbors, and co-workers. It does not escape attention when persons travel from out-of-town and at some expense to be present for a funeral. This may be perceived as honoring the life of the deceased. Of course, close relatives, if they are physically and financially able, are expected to return home for a funeral.

I had a nephew who was in prison when his brother was shot and killed, and this same nephew, at a different time, was in prison when his mother died. I have seen incarcerated persons in handcuffs or leg cuffs, attended by a guard, at the funeral of a parent. Appeals are often made to prison authorities for an imprisoned person to be released under guard to attend the funeral of a close relative. All appeals are not answered favorably.

Another nuance to the matter of attendance is the presence of ministers in the pulpit. If the funeral is in a church, the pastor's presence sends an important message of support to the family. There are occasions when a scheduling conflict precludes the pastor's attendance if the pastor is out of town. Nevertheless, the absence of the senior pastor is duly noted even when understood. I have known of pastors who were conducting out-of-town revivals who returned to eulogize a church member and flew back to the seat of the revival. This gesture on the part of the pastor is long remembered by family members.

Attendance is also affected by the day of the week for the funeral. Funerals may be held any day of the week, depending on a host of factors, including availability of the church or chapel, travel schedules of out-oftowners, and work schedules. Night funerals, though less frequent, are an option for those who cannot take off from work.

It has been my experience that there are ministers who show up at funerals hoping for an opportunity to speak. In some Baptist churches, the pastor may invite each minister in the pulpit to offer expressions of comfort to the family. I have seen these turn into short sermons. Some pastors are trusting that someone in the audience will remember them when or if a pulpit comes open. In a more brash move, I have seen pastors at a high-profile funeral of a senior pastor distribute their business cards on the parking lot.

I remember a funeral in which I was to preside and preach the eulogy. The deceased was someone who had been in and out trouble with the law. Police cars were in the parking lot and on the street just in case there was any gang retaliation. As I entered the pulpit, two senior ministers were already seated. I later discerned that they were there to ensure that things were done "decently and in order." The audience was made up primarily of young adults. During the service, a soloist began to sing an appropriate song but not a church song. The audience expressed their grief through loud wails and tears. The two older ministers in the pulpit began yelling at me to sit her down. I thought one of them might have a heart attack because the rejection was so visceral and vocal. I gestured with my hand for them to cease their antics; I was in charge, not them.

Location

I grew up in an era when the majority of funerals were held at a church. Now funerals may be held either in a church or in a funeral home chapel. In my hometown of Marshall, Texas, a third venue for funerals is a building owned by the Texas-Louisiana Baptist Association, commonly referred to as "The Association Building." Funerals at funeral home chapels are convenient in the sense that the body is already there. Convenience is even greater when the cemetery and the site of the funeral are on the same grounds. During my childhood, when funerals were held in the church, it was not only the family's funeral; it was the church's funeral, which meant that the choir was in attendance, ushers were at their post, and the deacons and Mother's Board were in their usual seats. Whether the site is a chapel or a church, if the deceased is a veteran and is being buried at a veteran's cemetery, the time limit is already set by the schedule of burial.

A family's decision to have the funeral at a church or at a funeral home is sometimes driven by whether or not the deceased was unchurched. In his autobiography *With Head and Heart,* Dr. Howard Thurman tells the story of how his grandmother had to intercede when the pastor of the church refused to allow his father to be funeralized in the church. From the pastor's perspective, Thurman's father did not know Jesus, and, therefore, it was not appropriate to have a church funeral for someone who was not a true member of the church. It took some persuasion by the grandmother for Thurman's father to be buried out of the church.

Mistress of Ceremonies

I grew up with the tradition of a funeral being presided over by the pastor and a "Mistress of Ceremonies." Either the pastor or the family may ask a particular woman to be the lay presider at the funeral. Whatever honor this person may feel bestowed upon her, the responsibility is to read the Order of Service and offer announcements on behalf of the family. The name of the Mistress of Ceremonies appears on the printed program. She does not join the procession but is already at her post when the service begins.

Emotional Release

Grief-stricken relatives and friends are free to express their pain and sorrow during the Wake and at the funeral. I have seen persons collapse into the casket. I have heard family members talk aloud to the deceased. I have seen persons so angry with God for taking their loved one until they verbally assault God—even curse—and refuse to be consoled. I have seen persons being physically forced by other family members to come into the sanctuary to face the reality of the death of their loved one. I have seen people fall out and have to be carried out by the ushers in a stretched-out position. Funerals in which family members and friends carry on in this manner are referred to as "a sad funeral."

In speaking with funeral home directors and morticians, I have learned that there is a perceived relationship between funeral drama and drama in the life of the deceased. Also, I was told that there may be a connection between class and emotionalism at Black funerals. If there is drama in the funeral home director's office at the time of making business decisions, especially if that drama is not settled with life insurance or someone coming through to pay, then that drama is carried over to the day of the funeral.

Religious Expressions of Comfort

Family members have to decide if scheduled "Words of Comfort" on the program offer comfort or not. In this section I want to record some of the repeated sayings I have heard at Black funerals.

"God is too wise to make a mistake and too kind to be unmerciful."

"God doesn't make mistakes."

"One day God went walking in the garden of flowers, and decided He needed another flower in heaven's garden. So God looked over the balcony of glory and picked a beautiful rose for heaven's garden."

"God allowed this to happen. This is God's will, and we must submit ourselves to the will of God."

"God loved him or her more."

Quoting a piece from the Apostle Paul: "It is better to be absent from the body and present with the Lord."

I heard a Baptist preacher say to a grieving family: "She is not dead; she's on vacation."

"Your loved one is in a better place."

I attended a funeral in which the preacher, intending to make a joke, said: "That's just a shell (pointing to the casket), the nut is gone."

I have heard many "words of comfort" morph into words of discomfort.

Resolutions, Tributes, and Remarks

Church resolutions are designed to comfort the family in the knowledge that their loved one was active in the church and will be missed by the church. The resolution may state the deceased's ministry involvements. The resolution reflects the church's gratitude for service rendered as a disciple of Christ. Moreover, it is a homily that stresses theological themes of comfort and trust, and offers the church's support and availability to future needs of the family. A Church Resolution is often a template or a standard that is given at each funeral, with appropriate alterations. For churches that have many funerals where the template is used, it may be important for the pastor or a designee to write a fresh resolution for each celebration. This would express the church's personal attention to the family in acknowledgement of the specific contributions of the deceased to the church and community.

Not all resolutions are publicly read. In the church's decision to read a set of resolutions, the pastor should have already discerned and invited the best readers in the congregation to be members of a cadre of resolution readers. I have been to funerals where the reader of resolutions stumbled embarrassingly through this sacred part of the service. It is common for the reader to offer the following closing statement: "A copy of this resolution will be given to the family, and a copy kept in the church archives." For churches that have established archival records, this is a matter of maintaining an important record for the family and the church. There are, however, some churches that make this traditional statement out of habit but do not have a systematic means of keeping and guarding the records of the church for posterity.

It is a common practice for the reader of the resolutions to acknowledge receipt of the many resolutions rather than read them all. It is understandable that in addition to the resolution of the church where the deceased held membership, for a resolution to be read from the church where the deceased held previous membership. Funerals of a community leader may have an extended time of sharing resolutions and/or tributes. While these statements of representation are important, the reading of many other resolutions and tributes can be taxing on a congregation.

In addition to a family member offering a tribute for the family, designated persons are sometimes invited to offer remarks. I have witnessed four or five designated persons offer tributes that were quite time-consuming. I concluded this is because they were not given a specific time limit, e.g., four minutes. Without these time markers, tributes have taken as much time or more than a sermon. Funerals that have an open mic time can be challenging both to the waiting congregation and to the Officiating Minister who says repeatedly that the time limit for remarks is two or three minutes. The two to three-minute limit is justified as given out of deference to the family. It is hard, though not impossible, for most speakers to stay within the time limit. A prepared remark that has been practiced is the key to staying within the time limit. Many people get in line to speak who don't know what they are going to say until they are in front of the microphone.

In traditional Black Baptist churches, the period of remarks begins with the pastors or ministers in the pulpit. As stated earlier, there are ministers who attend funerals who are not scheduled on the program or connected with the host church or family. Some ministers go to funerals because it is a public space to be recognized, to be given an opportunity to speak, and, hopefully, if noticed for one's speaking skills, get invited to preach at a church.

From Death to Burial

Most Black funerals occur on the average between seven to ten days following the death of a loved one. It may be shorter if the deceased has made her or his wishes known, or if plans have been made in advance. Keeping the body out for as much as a week or more allows family members who are out of town to make arrangements to travel. Also, a family may delay burial to avoid the perception that the family was in too big of a hurry to bury their loved one. The time frame, furthermore, underscores the funeral as both a family and a communal event.

The Printed Funeral Program

The funeral program is a good source of family history. When done well, it records the stages of life of the deceased. It may include a photo of the deceased on the front or inside cover. In the absence of a photo of the deceased, a sketch of the Bible or flowers or praying hands is appropriate for the front cover. Many funeral programs include extensive color photos of the deceased with family members and friends.

In addition to photos, the program often includes a poem and/or short letters from one or two close family members. These are tangible expressions of the grief process.

Many funeral attendees gather several copies of the program for personal record as well as to send to family members and friends. It is now customary for the funeral home director to distribute the program nearer the start of the service lest they get grabbed up by funeral program collectors. The program is a treasured memento.

My stepfather was a collector of funeral programs. Due to his physical limitation, he would call around for someone to bring him a funeral program. Over the years he had a stash of programs. While he was in the nursing home, I went to check on the house. One of the items I noticed missing on the top dresser where he kept them was this treasured collection of programs. Someone else thought as much of them as he did.

A Parting View

Most Black funerals have a time for viewing the body before the service begins. It is the family's decision to have the casket open or closed before they are escorted into the sanctuary. I was scheduled to preside and preach at a funeral of a well-connected individual. I noticed some agitation as the family was lining up to walk in. I went to the funeral director to inquire if the family had decided to leave the casket open or to close it. That was the source of the agitation. So, I went to the head of the family for a decision, after which, I communicated the decision to the funeral director, and the service began.

The decision to have an open casket viewing at the end of the service or not is based on two considerations. The first is tradition. It is tradition to have an open casket viewing at the end so that the family can say one final goodbye and release even more emotions. The second is theological. Theologically, the question is: Why open the casket after the gospel of resurrection and new life has been celebrated? I have been a witness to only one circumstantial casket opening at a grave site. An elderly, disabled patriarch of the family was unable to attend the funeral. A family member put him in a wheelchair and brought him to the Committal Service. With the casket half-way in the grave, the spouse of the deceased asked the funeral director to open the casket in deference to their ailing patriarch, and this was done.

Collection of Money

I have participated in funerals in which the family was unable to pay the funeral home the full amount for the burial. An arrangement was apparently worked out. With the consent of the pastor, someone comes forward and makes an appeal to assist the family with the burial. In some cases, volunteer ushers come forward and distribute the collection trays. It is announced that the full amount will be given to the family to defray the cost. Perhaps the announcement should say that the full amount will be turned over to the funeral home director.

This scenario, first, calls for sympathy. No one in attendance, except for a few family members, may really know the extent of financial strain that the family endured leading up to the death of a loved one. It is possible for resources to be depleted, if not almost gone. In this case, family members ask the community to share the burden of paying for the funeral.

Secondly, this scenario lifts up the issue of funeral preparations. Insurance companies and some funeral homes have pre-need plans to help family members get ready for the inevitable. The reality is that even when some people know that they are going to die, they make no preparations. It is sad to say but some family members do not prepare for their own death because they have concluded that somebody in the family is going to take care of it one way or the other. Making funeral plans is a conversation every family should have.

I remember driving to Marshall, Texas to sit beside the deathbed of one of my sisters. Several of her friends were in the room with her. At some point I heard them talking about her funeral, and I turned to them and said, "My sister did not have any insurance. More than likely, we would have her cremated." The next morning after she died, I went to the funeral home to discuss my options. A friend of my sister's showed up uninvited and sat with me while I heard the funeral home director give me the options along with costs. While I am sitting there, someone from the front office comes in and hands me a note with a phone number and a name. Disregarding the note, I step out of the office to call my older sister to share with her the options and to make a decision. We decided on cremation and a memorial service at the funeral home chapel. After leaving the funeral home, I called the number on the note, and this person offered me two-thousand dollars toward the funeral. I declined her offer because my portion of the cost for a full funeral would have tripled, not to mention the cost of a required bronze headstone at the perpetual care cemetery where our family plot is located.

Invitation to Christian Discipleship

It is rare to experience a minister open the doors of the church at a funeral. The few times I have witnessed an invitation to accept Christ, empty chairs were folded and taken away. My sense is that the few times the invitation was offered, the minister assumed that the deceased lived a raggedy life, and therefore some of his or her friends in attendance must also be living shady lives. The invitation following the sermon was an opportunity for them to acknowledge the error of their ways, and accept Christ and his way. While an invitation to Christian discipleship is always right in itself, I question the timing of it at a funeral.

STUDY GUIDE

CHAPTER ONE

1. What qualities or attributes were needed by preachers and community members, being mostly unable to read and write, to organize a church shortly after emancipation?

2. What are your reflections on the practice of students being referred to as "scholars" in schools that were connected to churches?

3. List some contributions that the Black Church has historically made to the Black Community.

4. Many historically Black colleges were birthed out of denominational concerns for the education of young people. What are some contributions that Black colleges have made to society?

5. In this book three images of the Black Church are presented. What other images come to mind?

6. Is the image of the church as an army appropriate today?

7. What are your reflections on the assertion that church conflicts may be related to unacknowledged secrets?

8. What has been your personal experience with the concept of fictive kinship?

9. This book mentions that the word "Institutional" is in the name of some churches even today. Churches that incorporated this word understood their mission as involving social outreach. What are your reflections on this title?

10. Mention is made of the connection between Masonic lodges and Black churches. Many Masonic lodges were called upon to lay a church's cornerstone. Take a look at your church's cornerstone. Are there any Masonic emblems? What information is recorded on the cornerstone?

11. Share a personal story about the value of preparing in advance for church on Sunday. Were there restrictions on what you could and could not do on Sunday?

12. This book mentions an instance in which community members "begged each other's pardon" in preparation to partake of the Lord's Supper. Is there a biblical precedent for this practice?

13. Why do you think church attendance is higher on First Sunday in most Black churches?

14. What should be the purposes of a revival?

15. Reflect on the practice of having a "mourner's bench" and the activities that surrounded persons sitting on the mourner's bench.

16. Does an outdoor “muddy creek” baptism have any more significance than a baptism in an indoor pool?

17. In the Baptist tradition baptism is by immersion. What are other ways to be baptized in other church traditions?

18. In reading the Church Covenant, what key words or phrases stand out to you?

19. In studying the classic African American prayer, select and comment on at least three images or metaphors that are used.

20. Why do you think this prayer has survived for well over a century?

21. What are your reflections on having a white image of Jesus in today’s Black church?

22. Can you recall how you felt when you first saw a painting of a Black Jesus?

23. How would you respond to the claim that the image of a Black Jesus or a Bible with all Black images is racism in reverse?

24. How would you interpret the account in Exodus of the crossing of the Red Sea from an Africentric perspective?

25. This book mentions several protocols for establishing order in the church. Identify the ones with which you are familiar.

26. List at least three protocols in your own church.

27. The author gives several wise sayings or proverbs from his church experience. Which ones have you heard before?

28. What are some other wise sayings that you have heard in the church?

CHAPTER 2

1. What are your reflections on the Lord's Supper scene as illustrated on the front cover of this book? What do you think is going on?

2. Do you know of a Black Baptist church that used to or does engage in this Communion practice?

3. Are there other church practices of which you would like to know the social origin and/or theological meaning?

4. Several hypotheses are presented regarding the origin and meaning of the Communion practice in which the deacons hold up the Communion covering like a curtain. With which hypothesis are you in agreement and why?

5. With which hypothesis are you in disagreement and why?

6. What other reasons for this practice have you heard, if any?

7. What do you think an early generation was trying to say in using the word "Circament"?

8. Three pastors offer their reflections on the meaning of the practice at the Lord's Table. What questions do their reflections raise for you?

9. Read the sermon "No Flies Landing on the Table." Add phrases or lines to this sermon to indicate your participation in this preaching event.

CHAPTER 3

1. What special days does your church celebrate?

2. How is your church's history archived? Does the church have a designated historian or an active committee?

3. In your church how do men support Women's Day? Do you consider it appropriate for a male pastor to be in the pulpit on Women's Day?

4. Have you ever had the experience of hearing a man preach on Women's Day? Have you ever had the experience of hearing a woman preach on Men's Day?

5. How does your church emphasize Black history beyond February?

6. Reflect on the historical meaning of Watch Night.

7. Has your church ever had to deal with the issue of a dress code? What does dressing casually mean to you?

8. Have the stories and experiences of senior saints been systematically recorded in your church? How important is it for elders of the church to be assisted in writing their memoirs?

9. Who are the Church Mothers where you have membership? Interview one of them about their life experiences.

10. What percentage of the musical offering is made up of hymns? Is it still a value to teach hymns to youth? Why?

11. Find a hymn that you like and write your own lyrics, merging the social and the spiritual.

12. Discuss three of the leadership images.

13. What are other leadership images that you would add?

14. This book concludes with several features of Black church funerals. What has been your experience with some of the features mentioned?

15. Does your church offer opportunities for members to hear presentations on funeral plans, life insurance, costs of funerals, payment options, etc?

16. What are your reflections on a minister inviting persons to come and give their life to Christ following a eulogy?

17. Is there anything else you would like to share?

ABOUT THE AUTHOR

The Reverend Dr. Thomas Spann is an ordained Baptist minister who retired in 2018 as the Director of the Intern Program at Perkins School of Theology, Southern Methodist University, in Dallas, Texas. He was employed in the Intern Program for 30 years. Dr. Spann's previous employment includes service as a Reserve Chaplain, Carswell Air Force Base in Fort Worth, Texas; Instructor of Philosophy, Shorter College, North Little Rock, Arkansas; and Religion Professor at Jarvis Christian College, Hawkins, Texas.

Dr. Spann served as a faculty member of Faith Calls, a two-week theological academy in the summer for high school and college students, connected with Perkins School of Theology. In addition to his work in the Intern Program, Dr. Spann has been invited on several occasions to teach the course *Ministry in the Black Church.* He has been an instructor of Preaching for the Dallas Bible Theological Institute. He has taught hundreds of seminary students and pastors the art of theological reflection upon the practice of ministry. Dr. Spann has served as a guest preacher and speaker on numerous occasions.

Upon retirement from SMU, Dr. Spann was called to serve as the Interim Pastor of the First Christian Methodist Evangelistic Church in Dallas, TX.

Dr. Spann attended the public schools in Marshall, Texas; received his Bachelor of Arts, Bishop College, Dallas, Texas; Master of Divinity, Princeton Theological Seminary, Princeton, New Jersey; and Doctor of Ministry, SMU, Dallas, Texas.

He is an *associate member* of St. Luke "Community" United Methodist Church in Dallas, while maintaining his ordination in the Baptist Church. He was baptized and ordained at the Pine Bluff Baptist Church in Karnack, Texas, under the leadership of Rev. Joseph Cooper.

He is married to Cynthia Hunter Spann. They have a daughter, Monique Spann Redmon, a son Thomas Spann, Jr., and four grandchildren.